Publisher: www.rronews.com

Printed in the United States.

Brian Tramel can be reached by visiting the following website:

www.rronews.com.

or by e-mail at:

brian_tramel@yahoo.com

# THANK YOU FROM BRIAN TRAMEL

----I am the guy who takes all this stuff that we worked on all year long and puts all the important things into this yearbook. I am also the one who posts about 95 percent of all the material that is read every day by more than 2000 readers on www.rasslinriotonline.com. I have told many people over the years that the site and these books are a "labor of love" for the wrestling business. Below are people that I would like to thank because the site or books would not be possible without them.

-Brian Thompson – He is my best friend to ever come out of the wrestling business. Thank you for your support and for being a friend. Thank you for being there when I need you and not asking for anything in return!!

-Misty Belly – Thank you from the bottom of my heart for taking the time to edit this book!! I am sorry the Colts lost, but we had a good day editing!!

-To my many columnists – Maxx Corbin, Greg Anthony, Pokerface, Downtown Bruno, Eric Wayne and Gene Jackson. If it wasn't for such a great staff putting out columns, I would sometimes have nothing to post. Thanks to each one you for your hard work.

-Tia Blaylock – Thank you for all the photos and for contributing them to this book. I can't say how much your photos are appreciated and how much they help the quality of this book.

-To the visitors to RRO!!! We have had more than 3.4 million hits in less than a five year history. Thank you!!

-To YOU for buying this book!!

-To all the workers in this area – you guys are living the dream!!!

-And finally, to my family – Kayte, Karly and Beth. I love you!! And my Mom, Glenda, who was brave enough to take me to wrestling for the first time in August of 1978!!

# This book is dedicated to Jeremy Wood.

*I never met Jeremy. All the people that knew him only had good things to say about him. They said he LOVED wrestling and just wanted to be part of it.*

*Brian Tramel*

## About the Author and Editor

### Brian Tramel

Brian Tramel is the owner and operator of www.RasslinRiotOnline.com.

Tramel has been around the wrestling business for the better part of 30 years. He began as a wrestling fan, and then became a journalist, wrestler, manager and promoter.

During his stint as a manager, Tramel was known as "Coach BT," carrying a clipboard as a weapon. The gimmick was a spinoff of John Tolos' "Coach" gimmick from the early 1990's in the World Wrestling Federation.

Tramel owned and operated a small promotion called Chaotic Championship Wrestling, which held live events throughout the Mid-South during the early part of the new millennium. After selling the promotion, Tramel returned to managing. He ended his active managing career and, in 2006, developed the RasslinRiot website, bringing his involvement in wrestling full circle as his first days physically in wrestling were as a "dirt sheet" writer.

The website has grown in popularity, leading to Tramel and Brian Thompson working together on the autobiography of wrestling journeyman Dusty Wolfe, the re-release of Bruno Sammartino's autobiography, several yearbooks focused on the Mid South and other future projects.

Tramel lives in Steele, MO and has three daughters – Kayte , Karly and Beth.

### Misty Belly, Editor

Misty Belly graduated from Texas A&M University. She has a Bachelor's Degree in English with a minor in Business and a Certificate of Technical Writing. She has worked for Shirley Publications as an Editor, and as Editor-in-Chief of "The Shadow Knows", a monthly publication of the Shire of the Shadowlands. She also spent many years in the desktop publishing department of the Jonesboro, AR Kinko's. Many samples of her work can still be found on signage and business cards in the area.

Currently working as a massage therapist in her own small business, A New Vitality located in Jonesboro, AR, Misty continues to hone her editing/desktop publishing skills by producing the marketing materials for her business as well as several others for friends and family members.

Misty was introduced to wrestling by none other than Brian Tramel himself. She saw her first match at NEW, where she was amazed at the athleticism and dedication of the wrestlers. She is honored to be asked to be part of the great effort at RRO to strengthen the "business" in the local area.

Go to http://rroawardsrace.blogspot.com/2011/01/yearbook-2010-web-companion.html for all references to *Yearbook 2010 Web Companion.*

### JANUARY

-Standing room only for the 1.02.10 EPW show with EPW Tag Team Champions Pure Destruction (Cody & Brody Hawk) defending against JR Mauler & Cassanova Kid.

-EWE "Aftermath" results.

-----Photo of Christian Jacobs after beating Greg Anthony for the EWE Title is in January photos. This is CJ's first singles title since a run with the Chaotic Championship Wrestling Mid-Southern Title in 2001-02. He has been primarily a tag team wrestler all his career. A scheduled Jacobs vs Dustin Starr feud never materialized due to Starr having commitments outside the wrestling business leading to EWE bringing in Greg Anthony to set Jacobs up to proverbially "take the ball." EWE is a company that always has a good roster and decent [though sometimes questionable] booking, but has not had big crowds over the last year. [They were nominated for Booker of The Year 2009] Jacobs is being put into a position to carry the company and get the attendance level up with him as champion. And as I have said in the past, "Picture Perfect" gets one of the biggest pops in this area, but can the pop = money? Jacobs received 3 nominations this year [2009] with two in the tag team division, and one in the Horizon. Horizon is an award that represents the WWE/TNA potential of a worker. Jacobs shone in September 2009 with four straight [***] or better bouts and with RRO tagging him as "Mr. September".

Complete Results:

Jon Michael over Cody Melton in a flag match.
JR Manson over Brandon Espinosa
Rude over Shane Rich
Christian Jacobs over "The Golden Boy" Greg Anthony to become the new EWE Champion
Team DK over Team EWE for Derrick to win total control of the company

-Dustin Starr commits to RCW and the first show is announced.

----Let me go on record in saying, as I have said to a few of you in private - if this promotion is not a success, it will not be from the guys not doing it the RIGHT way. I am privy to some of the inner workings of this promotion - add up the knowledge, the talent, and the advertising - they have it all going for them.

-DCW gets a new name.

----Dyersburg Championship Wrestling is now being called Mid-America Championship Wrestling, which is a name that has been used in the past in the area when Sir Mo booked.

-Tim Edwards beat Jason Vaughn to win MACW Title and "High Society" [Oz/Blaine Devine beat Brian Steele/Ike Tucker to win MACW Tag Team Titles. 1.01.10

-Coach's Corner "Contracts" is posted. 1.07.10

Contract: *An agreement between two or more parties, especially one that is written and enforceable by law.*

----My first edition of Coach's Corner this year, I want to touch on a subject that has become passing across my desk the last few weeks. Apparently two companies in this area have offered contracts to performers. Some even included exclusivity for the talent to stay with a certain company, or to stay away from other companies. And since I find this both stupid and smart, I had to write on it.

----First, let me state, that no one from either company has called me and said, "Hey we are offering contracts." Actually no worker from either company has told me this – so don't go through your dressing rooms looking for a spy. I know this from people that know people – ok.it is hearsay and I am going with it as commentary. So, just for the sake of this story, let's just go with the old comic mark thing "What if?" and go with it as fact.

----First, STUPID!!! How can a company offer or demand the workers sign a contract in the condition professional wrestling is in this area?? How will the guys benefit from something like this?? And, honestly, I do know there are promoters out there that make little or NO money, but if it was any other business would you continue to put money in it when it is failing?? That is where you get the hobby thing going and well, that is another column all together. The boys benefit how in signing a contract that says, "I will work for you only, keep my mouth shut about inner workings [aka don't tell BT], and I will show up to do x-amount of shows?" Is that a valid thing to sign?? It sounds real one-sided when it comes to the promotion/wrestler aspect. Why would you limit a wrestler from working more than one promotion?? Or actually say he cannot work for a certain promotion?? Especially when most groups run just 52 shows a year. The most would be a group like IWA, who runs [with TV] over 60 shows a year. If you are getting paid a DVD [that joke never gets old] or working for $5 from a shady [not Jamie – that one never gets old either..lol] promoter, then how is it going to benefit you to have them say you can only work here and not there??

----Second, SMART!! Yes, smart in the sense of, if the contract is to benefit both parties, then it can help you on any level. Let's say I am the promoter, I am running over 60 shows a year. I want a performer at ALL of them, but I also don't want him out there whoring himself out at the backyard show jobbing. As a worker, then I am guaranteed a certain amount of dates for a certain amount of money. Yes, you as a worker should make sure that it benefits you. That is where the smart part of this comes in and it can be a good thing. If you are only going to work for one promotion, then you must figure in the dates you will lose from not working other promotions. If you sign that contract, then you should ask for more money guaranteed, since they are asking for you to perform for just them. So say you are getting $25 per date now, then you should at least get a free DVD and an extra 40% more money.  If the promotion is doing TV, then a contract really might even be a smarter thing to do for the promotion – if you are a star there and get jobbed at the $5 place, then why would they want to use you??  If they are paying for TV, they are investing something in you, and it would only be smart for them to ask you not to make yourself look bad.

----All and all, the contract can either be stupid or smart for the promotion/worker.  Never sign anything without reading it first.  Make sure that both parties are going to benefit.  I suggest a short term – 3 months of dates with a guarantee amount of money total.  And remember, promoter and worker – you sign the agreement – it is considered law abiding and that means – someone could take you to court to make you uphold your end of the deal.

**-Alan Steele debuts for TCW in Fort Smith, AR.**

**-IWA announces that it will be on Memphis TV again, but fails to return in January.**

**-Austin Lane retains the ASWF Title in a "Fatal Fourway" vs Idol Bane, Demon X and Tommy Wayne hitting Wayne with a spear to win. 1.16.10**

**-The Straight Flush by Pokerface is posted. 1.19.10**

**Can business ever pick back up?**

I guess that is the $10,000 question.  But before I answer that, let's take a brief look at the business as it is now, at least on the local scene.  In the local area, on a weekly basis you have close to 10 shows running a week, give or take a few.  In one area, the Tennessee area, you got pretty much the same guys working the shows.  In the Arkansas area from what I hear you don't have as much of the "same face syndrome".  Up until a couple of months ago, we had two companies running on Memphis local TV.  It could have been the Saturday Morning Wrestling Wars, yeah right.  One company I used to work for, well actually I've technically worked for both companies.  That Saturday morning block of programming, I think, should've "made business pick up", but it didn't.  Which doesn't surprise me.  Here's why.

One show would run old footage, that nobody gives a f$%^ about.  The other featured wrestlers that nobody gives a f#$@ about.  If I offend anyone then too bad.  This is just my opinion.  Company #1 had the resources to do what Ring of Honor does, hell even what TNA does.  But it didn't.  The company would bring in "superstars" and still never drew in any extra fans.  I will say one time, I think maybe in '04 or '05 they had almost 7000 fans attending events in The Mid-South Coliseum.  That number dropped 83%.  WTF!!!!!!!!!  If you analyze it, the company never really thought outside the box as far as matches and promoting.  I'm not Don King by any means, but when your attendance drops from 7000 down to 400, somehow, somewhere, Houston, there is a problem.  When the "superstars" came in, the local talent got no rub whatsoever from them.  Again if what I'm saying is not true, look at the numbers.  I think the last chance Company #1 had at doing something big, is when the "Vicious One" came in, whom I always loved working with.

Now as for Company #2, they have a nice size roster from what I hear. They too have/had local TV. They have a lot of the guys I've known for years, some I like, some I wouldn't piss on if they were on fire. The company, from what I hear, lacks quality talent. I have only watched one show and I wasn't impressed. If you have a company with 30 guys on the roster, and out of that 30, maybe 4 of the guys are over with the crowd, can you say sinking boat? One guy on the roster talks so much s@#$, but couldn't out wrestle me if I had one arm and was in a coma. Then you got other guys who look like they could be meth addicts or weed heads, you know basically the backyarder look. At least take pride in your appearance. BUY SOME FREAKING GEAR! INVEST IN YOURSELF! Use your freaking weed/meth/beer money and buy a pair of tights DAMMIT! Anyway, this company has the potential of doing something, if they focus, are creative enough, and make a conscience effort to get the unknown guys over. But on the same token, you unknowns need to bust your ass to get over. Stop copying WWE and do your own thing!

Now for the other companies in the area. Like I said earlier, there is a "same face syndrome". That's why I stopped working for those companies. With the exception of a few names, nobody has been further than Newbern, TN. And it's been years since anybody has done any creative booking. You got damn near anybody booking these days. You had a kid that wasn't even legal to drive calling shots? He actually wanted to book me. I wish the f@#$ I had! I'm too much of an asshole to take instructions from a guy who still carries a lunch box. I just recently started having a few booking duties. I barely know what the f@#$ I'm doing, and I'm experienced. Now as far as the shows in Arkansas, I think the companies don't suffer from the SFS. The workers they have, for the most part, SUCK! And these dumbass promoters keeping booking them.

Now if I come off as a snob, I'm really not. I just take pride in what I do. So should everyone else. I've stated in a previous article, that I will pick veterans' brains; I continue to train in the ring; and I train in the gym. If I get out of line or need to improve on something, I'm humble enough to shut my mouth and take what ever advice or tongue-lashing I got coming. Just ask The Vicious One, The Dogg, or The Bad Guy. The business in the area could pick up once again. I don't see it getting back like it was in the days of old, UNLESS. it becomes one big company, which has all the best talent. There could be no BS outlaw promotion running with crappy wrestlers to kill the towns. I don't see TV really being a drawing factor unless you are running a commercial to promote your show. Weekly TV! HA! What a joke. Unless you are satisfied with only 400 fans showing up. Yes, that was sarcasm. If the promoters lived and breathed the business like they used to, or if the boys lived and breathed this business like they used to.... Man, wrestling would be heaven on earth. That's all for now. Until next time...Keep your pimp hand strong!

**-NEW announces TV debut.**

----It is official as of today that New Experience Wrestling will air on Mississippi television. The station, MYMS, will air episodes of NEW starting February 20, 2010 at 11:00am and will run for one hour. This comes just after RRO.com announcing NEW as the 2009 Promotion of the Year. NEW is owned by Nightmare Ken Wayne and runs every Friday night in West Memphis, Arkansas with a bell time of 8:00 pm and tickets are only $5.00. Be sure to check them out every Friday night and every Saturday Morning at 11:00am.

**-Coach's Corner "Wrestling On TV" posted. 1.21.10**

----By the end of February, this area will start airing three wrestling TV programs. If IWA does start again this week, it will be joined by NEW and RCW on February 20th with their weekly shows. All three shows will be in different markets and not competing with each other – Memphis, Jonesboro and Tupelo. I thought I would take this column to talk about the TV production, the talent and the booking – pros & cons of all three promotions.


IWA

-TV Production: This has to improve. Hire an announcer!! Get two cameras or at least move around with the one you have. Go out and get sponsors to help with improving the production. If you can get people to turn this show on again, you've got to give them something to make them want to come back to watch. I would actually try a studio feel, since it is in the Memphis market.

-Talent: Not sure who all is gone and who is all is still here. I am hearing that Tatt2, Malkavain, Michael Ward and Blalok are gone?? If so, then this weakens the roster. All those guys contributed to the show. You still have "Asylum", Seth Knight, Johnny Dotson, Bishop and Precious. I would consider these guys the top tier of the group. Dotson has been seen on Memphis TV and it has been proven he can have good to great matches. Knight's potential is "untapped" for TV and he should be pushed thru the roof. The same thing can be said about Bishop. Precious makes the list as he is a solid worker and is entertaining at times. "Asylum" are one of the top teams in this area and if put in the ring with the right opponents can provide "oh s**t" moments. V-Man is probably the only other guy I would consider even pushing on this show and he would be good as a monster type character.

-Booking: They have to get their book established so they can have ideas that are episodic and mean something. If you are building for a big show that you want people to pay and attend – you must push toward that at all times, giving people the matches and such. But, you also got to give them the results afterwards. If you don't, then it does not mean anything. Also – do not do angles backstage that the viewer never sees. There were way too many of them.

NEW

-TV Production: This show will be the best production of any wrestling show you have seen in this area. It has a great studio feel and the show is produced with more than one camera and post production that will make anyone envious. The announcers are two of the best in the area, are very familiar with the product, and they believe in it. This group has spent more than a year getting ready for this opportunity. They are going to be heads above everyone in this department.

Talent: They have some of the best in the area.  Pure wrestlers in the building that they tape – you can not get a much better crew for this style. The standouts are guys like Austin Lane and Alan Steele, who I consider both very marketable even to the casual fan.  Guys like Eric Wayne, Kid Nikels, Shawn Reed or Justin Smart, who have tremendous talent, will be given the opportunity to see if they can get over with the masses.  I do feel they will have to add some other faces and maybe some familiar ones like Greg Anthony, Derrick King or Dustin Starr – good workers that have "it", that can get the attention of people.  Will the unproven factor of some of the NEW guys actually improve their chances of getting over??

Booking: Ken Wayne and Alan Steele will be handling the bulk of this chore.  Wayne having experience in doing TV and Steele being on Power Pro [week in and week out] could not hurt a thing.  Both have good wrestling minds with Wayne more "old school" and Steele being younger, but probably a bit "old school" also.  Can the ROH style that they are so compared with sell to the masses in this area??  I think Wayne/Steele see the potential of presenting a show that features athletic contests, but I do not see them booking a show with no heels/babys.  I think it will be a mix of both and it should be fun to watch.

RCW

TV Production: I think they might be straddling the fence here.  They will not be the same level of production as say NEW, but I don't think they will be IWA either.  Let's hope not!!  TV will be filmed at the arena and be put in post production for a 30 minute show that will be sort of magazine format with an indy wrestling feel.  Well, that is what I am gathering from Thompson.  And Thompson will be doing the post announcing, so that will be top notch.  The two other shows have good time slots [11:00 AM for NEW and 12:00 Noon for IWA], but RCW will be stuck in the 1:00 AM slot.  Will that hurt them??  In the age of DVRs and the way they are getting the word out, it shouldn't.

Talent: Not one guy on this roster is not marketable to the masses.  Each of them have their own niche and know what they are doing.  They are the cream of the crop and if I was putting together a roster it would be hard not to include all these guys.  They have Wrestler, Tag Team, MVP Performer, Match of the Year participates, and it goes on and on.  And guys that might not be award winners but are going to be assets, such as Ron Rage, who was on some of the top weekly drawing cards in a feud last year – in Jonesboro, and Matt Riviera – on a lot of top shows and just a damn good performer.  From top to bottom – the best roster in the area and they haven't even run a show.

Booking: I have great faith in a guy like Brian Thompson.  He has a great young wrestling mind that can come up with some of best stuff to get people over.  He has Greg Anthony in to help, who has been on every booking committee to win Booker of the Year, since the start of this site.  He will book with an "old school" feel, but to say that does not work in this area – well when was the last time it was really done and done right on TV??  Terry Funk-Jerry Lawler??  Kevin White-Bill Dundee had a few TV shows in the days of this site that almost drew 100,000 viewers with "old school" booking.

----I am excited about having this much TV in the area.  I want all of them to succeed.  It will make it better for the workers as a whole.  My major concern for all three promotions would be that their TV is not on strong enough channels for the exposure to equal more people at the arena.  My Network is the weakest of the big networks, but it is accessible on Direct TV and Dish Network in your local area.  Jonesboro is local – you can get it on all major cable systems in the area and they are an ABC affiliate.  But, on the other hand, they are not on either Direct TV or Dish Network.

----All that said and done, I hope you have enjoyed my look at the TV production, talent and booking of all three promotions that are starting to air wrestling on TV.

**-TCW has 400 in attendance with Reckage & Romance (Matt Riviera & Jeff Jett) vs Alan Steele & Buddy Landel main event.  Go to *Yearbook 2010 Web Companion* for full results. 1.16.10**

**-TCW has 500 in attendance for sellout with Reckage & Romance (Matt Riviera & Jeff Jett) vs Midnight Gold (Bobby Eaton & Greg Anthony) with Brian Thompson on the show.  Go *Yearbook 2010 Web Companion* for full results. 1.23.10**

**-Tojo Yamamoto Jr receives 100 stictches after a match.**

**-Gene Jackson teams with Neil Taylor to beat Tony/Dabbs & A.N.T. 1.22.10**

**-Bill Dundee wrestles at EPW.**

**-Mama Say It Bees That Way Sometimes – Downtown Bruno posts Top 10 career moments.**

-My first day on Memphis television [1984]
-My first championship I managed somebody to win. [Hawaii 1983 – Superfly Tui – not Snuka]
-Getting the call to go to the WWF.
-Buying and owning my home and property outright! [hell, the business paid for it; right??]
-Main eventing in Wrestlemania 91.
-Eddie Marlin putting me in charge of the ticket sales and ring crew in 1988.
-Tojo Yamamoto buying me a Lincoln Continental in 1987.
-Robert Fuller teaching me how to A) Drive B) Swim and C) Drink excessively.
-Having a book of my life in the business published by Scott

And FINALLY - last, but not least – being a chosen member of the inner circle of New Experience Wrestling since it's inception, since DAY ONE

**-Lucky beats Pokerface to win the DCW Title.  Jonesboro, AR 1.23.10**

**-All local shows canceled due to snow and ice including RCW debut show.**

**-The East Arkansas News Leader reports Dustin Starr will be traveling to WWE Royal Rumble.** *After his match in Trumann Friday, Starr will begin his journey which will first take him to Atlanta, Ga., for the Rumble event. Then he will travel Monday to Nashville, Tenn., for the live Monday Night RAW event at Sommet Center before wrapping up the three-day trip in his home region of Memphis when WWE tapes it's SmackDown! and ECW broadcasts at the FedEx Forum Tuesday night.*

## JANUARY PHOTOS

**Top left clockwise: Christian Jacobs, RCW poster, NBW's Anarchy, Tojo gets stiches and Gene Jackson & JD McKay.**

## FEBRUARY

-NBW draws 270 fans for Vendetta. 2.06.10  Go to *Yearbook 2010 Web Companion* for full results.

-Pokerface beats Lucky for DCW Title.  Jonesboro, AR 2.06.10.

-Flash Flanagan returned to EWE for a few shots.

-Wayne's World posted by Eric Wayne. 2.10.10

"Achieving Perfection"

On February 1 and 2, I had the opportunity to work for WWE in Nashville and Memphis.  I wasn't the only one but I thought I'd share what I took away from the experience.

Even though none of the extra talent made TV appearances, the learning experience was invaluable.  Besides being able to workout in their ring, watching the other guys workout and work on different techniques was just as good as the exposure of being on TV.  For around two hours, we either had the chance to have a match or simply watch and listen. Even though I'm proud of the two matches I had, it's hard to accept that it wasn't WWE quality.

After listening to the advice being given to the TV talent, I realized exactly how much perfection means to these guys.  Not to say I didn't before, but it's a reminder how much everyone there strives to perfect EVERYTHING.  The talent in WWE, even the ones that we might think aren't that good, are damn good.  It might not come across on TV but watching the workouts proves just how hard these guys work.

Achieving perfection seems to be the motto in WWE and it should be the motto for everyone that gets into the business.  Unfortunately, it's not.  The motto seems to be "just enough to get by" which is sad when you think about it.  A lot of the "wrestlers" today started because of what they saw on TV.  The biggest difference between what was on TV and what's at pretty much every show on the weekend, is a lack of dedication and heart.  WWE is full of guys with the biggest heart and dedication to be the best.  You can only say that for a handful of guys around here, or anywhere for that matter.

When it comes to this business, I can't help but notice that at shows on the weekend, it's ok to be bad at your craft.  Almost like it's a rib on the audience to make them watch how bad a certain wrestler is instead of remedying the problem by kicking that person not only out of the ring, but out of the business until they learn their craft.  Does no one realize the reason WWE and a select few promotions are drawing?  It's because they don't expose the business when they have a match! But go to pretty much ANY show on the weekend and what do you see?  Guys that call themselves wrestlers, trying to have a match.  Hell, I have a driver's license...but I'd never attempt driving in a NASCAR race.  Why should wrestling be any different?

Maybe it's because there aren't many people today that actually want a career in wrestling. They just want to say they've wrestled. Well that's a horrible reason to get in this business and a slap in the face to some of us because you're only making it harder for people that take it seriously. You're making it harder for companies to draw because no one wants to see you in the ring. You're making it harder for the audience to sit there and wait for a good match, or even a good wrestler to come to the ring. No one pays to watch "wrestlers" pretend they're wrestling. No one pays to watch something you consider a hobby. They pay to watch professionals. Which is exactly why WWE and TNA draw like they do. Because they hire professionals.

It all comes down to this, if what I've said has upset you...I don't care. If you are booked on the weekend and you consider wrestling a hobby, don't show up! If you have been "wrestling" for 15, 20, 25 years and you're no better than the day you started or a guy with LESS THAN A YEAR of experience, don't show up! No one will miss you and the house won't go down. If anything it'll go up because that's one less bad wrestler on the card. It all comes down to achieving perfection, which is something you're not willing to do. If you wrestle once or twice a week, for 10 minutes because it's all your stamina will allow...QUIT! No one will miss you. And if anything, people will applaud you for realizing YOU are the one that hurts this business. All because achieving perfection is something you've never considered.

**-LSD Walk Out on ASWF: The Story.**

----After reporting that LSD walked out on ASWF, RRO received the following e-mail explaining the situation.

While training with a "trainee" of David Walls and Tommy Wayne's. We were running the gauntlet with him. He was getting blown up and wasn't getting up to finish the round of moves. We told him that there isn't time in a match to stop and take a break. The "trainee" also said we had to take it easy on him because he's a seizure patient. Deadly Dale said, "Well maybe you're in the wrong business". Cody Only may have used some "colorful" language to get their message across. The so-called "trainee" took offense to Only's coaching and some other words were exchanged...the "trainee" then said he was quitting and attempted to get out of the ring and was kicked out of the ring by Deadly Dale. The "trainee" threatened to call police for being kicked by Deadly, then proceeded to say we were being too rough on him and we were disrespecting him. To which Cody Only replied, "You don't deserve any respect! Respect has to be earned! I was s**t on the whole time I trained, and for the next two years after that! You're nobody special!" Another witness to the incident told LSD that David Walls was at the concession stand watching the entire incident and walked away when his name was mentioned.

The "trainee" then went running to David Walls. David then comes out to the ring bitching at Tommy Wayne saying he's the only one that's supposed to be working with this guy. He's acting all pissy about this and is clearly talking about US, but the whole time does not even look at us. This was the thing that topped off a whole pile of stupid stuff that's been stacking up for a while. The fact that he chose this guy, who is mentally challenged and the biggest mark in the building, over us was total disrepect. Deadly responded, "Well F**k it, we'll leave!" At this point, Idol stopped David as he was walking toward the front door and tried to explain the situation. David spouted off, "We don't need you!" in response to Deadly saying, "I'm out of here!" This was the point where Idol had had enough and said, "F**k it, we're out of here!" So we grabbed our bags and left right then.

This was the final straw in a long list of disrespectful and idiotic things that we have had to endure during our tenure there at ASWF. David Walls, plain and simple, DOES NOT belong in the wrestling business. If he actually had any clue about this business then maybe he wouldn't be losing three of his most over guys due to a "trainee" that WILL NOT do anything in this business and shouldn't. David X has never trained to wrestle. So how does he have any clue of what the training process for this business should be like? When training, aren't you supposed to push the trainees to see if they have the guts to make it in this business. Always thought that was how it was done.

For the people that continue to attend ASWF shows...please know that and every time that he puts on his Demon X mask and steps into the ring, he disgraces this business and showing his total lack of respect for the boys and the business. In conclusion, we want to once again say thank you to all the LSD fans in the Tuckerman area for your support and watch for updates on where LSD will be appearing next.

**-Rodney Grimes Scores Big!**

---- The two biggest shows at this point in the ring are from Rodney Grimes' CWA. Grimes was considered one of the top indy promoters in this area around the start of the site and placed in the Top 10 of shows in Yearbook 2007. He has pretty much disappeared from the scene for the last two years, but looks like he is back with a vengeance. This is only February, but those two shows could easily be in the top 5 shows of 2010. I am hearing anywhere from 600 to 1,000 people in Ripley, MS [Go to *Yearbook 2010 Web Companion* for full results] and 700 in Savannah, TN [Go to *Yearbook 2010 Web Companion* for full results], but was told it was a big crowd. I did get a yahoo im message that read, *"2 awesome cwa legends shows omg the people"* [in reference to big crowds].

----Grimes has re-merged in the promoting game in a totally different environment than when he left. Memphis Wrestling was drawing some of the bigger gates and guys like Jerry Lawler, Bill Dundee and others had a TV outlet that was an average of more than 59,000 viewers. Just a minor mention of some of Grimes' shows would be a boost in the attendance. No TV exposure and just hard selling advertising seems to have paid off with maybe the fans getting an "absence makes the heart grow fonder" attitude and going out to support the Legends.

----These shows were packed with Lawler, Don Bass, Bill Dundee, Buff Bagwell [who has really proven to be a draw in this area], Dutch Mantell and a host of undercard guys featuring some of the local talent. The only question is, "Will the nostalgia gimmick work if these guys do another round of shows?" Fans usually have a vision of what their legends *were* and not what they actually are now.  They get to see what old age and the road has done to to them, then going out to the shows is a one time thing.  The key would be to not use the same people [legends] over and over and capitalize on local talent.

**-Arena Report: NEW West Memphis, AR 2.12.10.**

-----Kevin Charles beat Dan Matthews… Dustin "Five" Starr used the tights to beat Mike Anthony… Austin Lane beat Justin Smart… Eric Wayne/Kid Nikels beat Alan Steele/ Shawn Reed

Full Report and Notes go to *Yearbook 2010 Web Companion.*

**-SAW's "Unfinished Business" draws 1000+ fans for show in Nashville, TN featuring a lot of Memphis based talent. 2.13.10 [Go to *Yearbook 2010 Web Companion* for full results]**

**-NEW debuts on MY MS.**

**-Dustin Starr wrestles last show in area before leaving for WWE Developmental in Florida. West Memphis, AR 2.19.10**

**-Terrance Ward announces he is leaving ASWF also, but returns.**

**-Jeremy Moore wins NBW Title in Battle Royal. 2.23.10**

**-PWA show in Vanndale, AR features** The "Asylum" [Psycho/Pappy] vs. "Picture Perfect" [Christian Jacobs/Jon Michael].

**-Danny B Goode Shoots!**

**----D-Rock posted the following on www.wrestlingnewscenter.com**

Tonight, at the XOW show that took place in Hernando, several strange events occurred, involving Danny B.

First, before the match was getting ready to begin, Danny went off on the mic, blasting the promotion for not having the cage that was advertised and claimed they were cheating the people. Referee Chris P. Fries explained that they had a flat and could not deliver the cage in time for the match.  Danny B. made some disparaging remarks to Chris P. and got right in his face, telling him, "This is a shoot!"

Later, after the end of an incredible and crazy main event, Danny B. hit Mickey Ray with several stiff chair shots and challenged any of the guys in the back that had something to say to come on down to the ring.  Syn, who was watching the show in the crowd, came to check on Mickey Ray. Syn told Danny, "That's enough", but Danny kept going off on his tirade.  The fans left because things were getting a bit too heated.

XOW's Tony Watts asked me if I would post his response to Danny B's strange situation that transpired Saturday night.

**----RRO talked with Mickey the morning after the event.**

----I had the chance to talk with Mickey Ray via cell phone about the situation with Danny B Goode from XOW's show yesterday morning. Ray had just turned on Goode in the bout and he planned to run in, bump a few times and leave Goode in the ring to do his end of night dance. He stated that Danny hit him very hard in the back of the head first and that was not planned. He then went on hitting him in the back and leg with the chair. Goode swung the chair holding it by one leg and Ray ended up with a big knot on the back of his head. When I asked if it was a work, he said, "Not this time brother."

----So, all the workers and fans in the area will go in conspiracy mode, saying this is a huge work and not a shoot. And, honestly I thought the same thing. But, let's go back to the lesson learned for the Bishop/Brian Christopher incident from last year. If these two guys work each other in the very near future, then it was a work. If you never see them in the ring against each other or even on the same shows with each other, then it was a shoot. Also, ask yourself – who are they working if it is not a shoot?? Wrestling News Center and RRO?? If so, then Mississippi wrestling promoters are stupider than I thought they were. On the site, I talked about a "shoot" angle that Jon Michael/Derrick King did on Saturday night at EWE. It was an angle and they were not working me backstage after the angle, because the guys that read this site are not going to equal money at the box office.

----And I will go on record, and I pretty much said the same thing about Brian Christopher, if you are a promoter in this area and you use Danny B Goode..well…you are stupid. Goode apparently went off on the whole crew backstage and never apologized to Ray. This business is based on getting in the ring and trusting your opponent. Even with the worst situations we have had with Eric Wayne/Greg King Jr and Syn/Jason Reed – those guys going in the ring trusted one another. And if you talked to all four of those guys right now, I can bet they would not have a problem working those same guys again. Ray would not be able to say that about Goode, because he could not trust him. Can everyone else just trust Goode and consider this an isolated incident?? I have worked with Ray on many occasions and it has always been a pleasure – one of the nicest guys in this area. I have worked with Goode once and it was a good experience also, but I have been told by many people in this area that Goode is hard to work with and doesn't like doing a job.

----On the flip side, if it is a work, then you guys should know better. This will not benefit anyone and actually just gives Goode a bad name. I was told there were a lot of workers in the crowd and when Goode dropped the "f-bomb" a few times and such, the crowd left unhappy. There is a difference in leaving the crowd unhappy [at the babyface] than leaving them wanting to kill the heel [DK/Michael angle].

**-Arena Report NEW West Memphis, AR 2.26.10**

-----Mike Anthony beat Jason Rose…Austin Lane/Eric Wayne beat Shawn Reed/Johnny Dotson …Nikki Lane beat Tasha Simone…Kevin Charles/Dan Matthews billed as "Prime Danger" beat "Midnight Gold" [Bobby Eaton/Greg Anthony]…Alan Steele beat Kid Nikels.

Full Report and Notes go to *Yearbook 2010 Web Companion*.

**-Arena Report: EWE Ripley, TN 2.27.10**

-----Tatt2 beat Gaylon Ray…"The Prodigies" [Rockin Randy/Dell Tucker] with Derrick King beat "Rhythm & Blues" [Ike Tucker/Brian Steele] with Rick Marx…Rude beat Tommy Redneck..Jon Michael beat Cody Melton...Flash Flanagan/Tommy Jones/JR Manson beat "LSD" [Idol Bane/Cody Only/Deadly Dale]…Christian Jacobs pinned Derrick King [****].

Full Report and Notes go to *Yearbook 2010 Web Companion*.

**-Ron Rage returns as a babyface to DCW.**

**-Derrick King is fired from EWE.**

----DK posted the following on his myspace.com account on Monday.  Apparently the building owner [JC] was unhappy with the "shoot" angle from Saturday.  This has been a back and forth battle with the owner and current EWE promoter, Stan Lee.  This stuff happens when a mark [JC] tries to run a wrestling promotion!!

*I was just informed that I was no longer needed in Ripley at EWE due to JC threatening to shut down the show.  I had fun while it lasted.*

## FEBRUARY PHOTOS

Top left top row: Mickey Ray and Danny B Goode

Middle left row: Eric Wayne and Dustin Starr

Lower left row: "LSD" /"Asylum" and Ron Rage

## MARCH

-RCW talent on KISS-FM radio in Jonesboro, AR to promote RCW debut.

-Arena Report: RCW Trumann, AR 3.05.10

----Christian Jacobs beat Seth Knight….Austin Lane beat Bishop…Ron Rage beat Matt Rivera…Jon Michael Worthington beat Cody Melton…"Hot Topic" [Derrick King/Stan Lee] beat "Midnight Gold" [Bobby Eaton/Greg Anthony].

Full Report and Notes go to *Yearbook 2010 Web Companion*.

*-Business Is Good!!  What is Right With The Wrestling Business!* **Posted.**

----This area was packed with wrestling fans this weekend with people coming out in big numbers. Henderson, TN had 1000+ packed in the building Friday night with Memphis Wrestling stars. Luxora, AR had 517 people for MCW with Koko Ware and Sid Vicious.  Vicious proves again to be a draw for this area.  Brian Thompson reported 78 paid for RCW debut and I am guessing over 100 in the building.  Not a great number, but I think it was real good considering the last wrestling show in Trumann, AR drew about 7 paid.  That group has a higher ticket price with most groups having to draw in the 130+ number to even come close to their gate.  I talked with the EWE office last night and they were in the 150+ range [drawing off that angle from last week-DK did show up last night also!!] and RRO was live in Newbern, TN for NBW with close to 130+ in the building.

----An almost four year rant on my part of the collation of good workrate = good wrestling = good gates seems to finally be paying off for the area.  I have been to five shows in the last few weeks and the workrate in this area is far above what it was when this site started.  The understanding of putting a match together and doing different things for the same results and just the level of psychology even for the young guys is good.  I have written the word "solid" in my notebook so many times in the last few weeks.  This area is full of guys willing to work hard and go out and try different things.  The level of talent that was at the RCW show was a perfect example of taking all the best workers in the area and turning out good matches - stuff at the level that fans are not used to getting in a town like Trumann, AR.  Thanks to all of you - give yourself a pat on the back!  For us that talk so much about "what is wrong with the wrestling business", it is really good to see it when things are being done RIGHT.

-MCW draws 517 in Luxora, AR with Bishop vs Frankie Tucker main event. 3.05.10. Results g o to *Yearbook 2010 Web Companion*.

 -Southern Wrestling Superstars draw 1044 paid for show in Henderson, TN.  Headlined with Jerry Lawler vs Bill Dundee. 3.05.10 Results g o to *Yearbook 2010 Web Companion*.

**-The Golden Circle "Power of the Internet" by Greg Anthony**

----I sent Greg a note when I got this edition and said to the extent, "Are you putting me over or insulting me here?" LOL He brings up some good points. I think the reason my opinion has so much merit is because of the same reason Greg says - he respects what I say, but does not always agree with me. I pride myself on having a unique view of the business - I still love the business as a fan, but I also know how stuff should be done. Overall I am going to praise someone I like [duh] over someone I don't like - but it is never based on "friendship" - it is based on what I consider their worth to the product. I am also able to see things that others in this area seem unable to - I see the mistakes I made in the past and try to help people that do the same stupid stuff. And, btw, after reading this I got a good laugh out of the "what it feels like to lock up with that individual", which is 100% true. I laugh because even though TGB is one of the most respected guys by his peers in this area, they always say to me, "He wants to call the whole match.." LOL But, on the other hand, the only good match I ever had in my life was a match TGB called for me.

I am amazed at how much the internet has influenced the world. I'm part of a generation that will be able to tell our kids about a time before the internet. It has changed the way we interact, converse and live. It's changed the way every business functions, even wrestling, hell.. especially wrestling. The changes have been both positive and negative. No matter which side of the fence you are on, you cannot deny the power of the internet.

Before anyone can point out the irony of me writing an article about the power of the internet while on the internet, let me say I am aware. Thank you, smartasses. But since you've got the ball rolling let's use rasslinriot itself as an example. The owner/operator of this site, Brian Tramel, is a friend of mine. He gave me one of my first bookings away from the federation that gave us our break. Since then we have become close friends.

Now I respect BT's opinion because he's a friend, not because he owns a website. You might be surprised how many people out there are determining their value based on his opinion. Now just because we're friends doesn't mean I agree with him 100%. We've disagreed about workers, matches, finishes and just wrestling in general. The power of the internet has defiantly taken his opinion's worth to another level.

The one thing is that BT can rave about a particular worker, but he doesn't know what it feels like to lock up with that individual. Someone that he likes may be, as we say, "Like Pulling Teeth". BT loves wrestling creatively and sometimes will give his thoughts on maybe how the booking should have been handled. What BT isn't , is in that locker room and aware the deciding factor of that booking decision.

I guess what I'm trying to say is don't pin your hopes and dreams on a website's opinion. Not this one or any other. Rather find several close friends in the business that you know, they know what they are talking about and they'll be honest with you and themselves. BT has praised me and openly disagreed with me in this forum. I've argued with his disagreements, and even some of his praises(although not publicly), LOL. I don't take it personally, because it's not personal. It's business and I've been a person that encouraged him to voice his opinion. What kind of hypocrite would I be if I told him to voice his opinion as long as it wasn't negative against me? What I'll tell anyone about critique or praise is consider the source.

**-Arena Report: NBW Newbern, TN 3.06.10**

---- Mark Justice/Kid with Mad Money Mike beat "High Society" [Blaine Devine/Oz]… Shannon Lee by reversal over Jason Reed to retain NBW High Risk Title… "Black Label Society" [Void/Robbie Douglas] beat J-Weezy/Jon "Biscuit" Robert…Jeremy Moore with Blaine Devine beat Shawn Reed with Coach BT to retain the NBW Title…Sarge O'Reilly with Billy Russ vs Mickey Ray – no contest.

For Full Report go to : *Yearbook 2010 Web Companion*.

**-Memphis Championship Wrestling draws 400 in Boliver, TN with Spelbinder winning a Battle Royal in the main event. 3.19.10.** Full Report and notes go to : *Yearbook 2010 Web Companion*.

**-Stan Lee leaves EWE.**

 ----Stan Lee, who has been booking this group since the change over from TLCW to EWE is gone. He is done with the promotion along with Derrick King, Cody Melton and a few more. Lee is forming a tag team with Chris O'Neal and will be called "High Stakes". They are taking booking in the area. The show will be booked by Christian Jacobs. I look for him and Jon Michael to do a lot of the EWE stuff from this point forward.

**-Arena Report:: Championship Wrestling Paragould, AR 3.20.10**

 ----Chris Day/Cold beat Snuffy/Jermey Spiker…The Enforcer beat Dr. Nemo Luv… Loose Cannon/Rik Burton with "Big Money" Frank Martin beat Triple D/Big Indian Quixote… Big Daddy LaFonce/Midnight Cowboy beat The Hambones…Tasha Simone/"Asylum" [Psycho/Pappy] beat Worm/Suicide/Adrian Banks [***3/4]…"East Coast Bad Boys" [C-Money/Serpent] beat Motley Cruz/Bishop.

Full Report and notes go to: *Yearbook 2010 Web Companio*.

**-Gene Jackson teams with Izzy Rotten to beat The "Asylum" [Pappy/Psycho] at TFW.**

**-Arena Report: DCW Jonesboro, AR 3.27.10**

 ----Genesis beat Rod Price…Ron McClarity beat Tejano Kid with Dominique…Southside Brawler beat Pimptacular…Purple Haze beat JD Kerry….Pokerface with Angel-Lena beat Marty Graw… Jazz beat Simply Luscious by DQ

Full report and notes go to: *Yearbook 2010 Web Companion.*

**-The Straight Flush with Pokerface.**

The State of the Business ( well locally):

Has anything changed much since my last gripe?  Ha, ha, I don't think it has.  Business as usual from what I gather.  It is, and probably will continue to be, the same old same with a few little fluctuations here and there.  Now it's time for my rant.

TV- As far as I know, four promotions are either on or about to be on some kind of television spot.  I guess for some reason these people actually feel that they can make money running a wrestling company.  I'm not saying that it's impossible, but the chances are slim and A-cup (think about it).  I've worked in many different places where they were "gonna or try to get TV".  Let's just say they aren't in business anymore.  It's more involved than most people think.  I should know, I've seen it done the right way and the wrong way.  I know some exposure is better than none, but it all comes down to the product.  I worked for a company over a year ago, that drew near the 400 paid mark on a semi regular basis.  That means a lot to me because I saw it grow from barely 100 paid to 400 in about 6 months.  That's a pretty big jump for an indy show.  True they did have a TV spot locally, but it was the hard work of the guys that did it, and I was proud to be part of it.  Again it's all about your product.  Honestly, I hope all these new television ventures succeed; I guess time will tell.  In one area that I work, at times there may be 3 companies running on the same weekend.  That's too many people trying to divide the pie.  And we wonder why no one is drawing.

Attendance - From what I hear at times the attendance is a little higher, I guess.  For most companies to draw they have to give away tickets, do a benefit, or some kind of special night attraction.  Now there is nothing wrong with that, we gotta do what we gotta do.  But if that's the only way we can draw, then something is wrong.  Sometimes special incentives are needed to stimulate or re- stimulate the fans' interest.  When it's all said and done, it's about the product and marketing.  One of the best advertising tools is word of mouth.  How do rumors spread?  If you can give the fans something that they'll be talking about for at least 3 days after the show, then you are on the right track.  To a certain point, that should be on the shoulders of the wrestlers as well as the promoters.  Do what's good for the business.  Be willing to be a sacrificial lamb for the company.  That doesn't mean to let yourself get buried, but try to keep the mindset that, at least at this level, this is a team sport.

Once again, I know my attempt to smarten the "boys" or the "office" is futile. You can't say I haven't tried. Nothing I gripe about or bring up is anything that I don't do myself. Anyone I've worked with or for can attest to that. Until then, we will continue to see the same old matches, with no creativity. The same weekend warrior wrestlers, who are afraid to get out of their comfort zone. We will continue to see the "babyface shine", heat spot, heat, double down, comeback, cutoff, and finish (YAWN!!!!!!!!!!!!) The same lame ass, boring promos that would put a dead man in a coma. We will continue hearing about mofos getting fired from one company and then jumping ship 30 miles down the road, just to kiss and make up 2 months later and make the whole thing an angle. Then do the s**t over again. We will continue to hear about mofos not wanting to do business because they are soooooo good and over. That's why I'm selective about the shows I do. Even the ones that "draw" 1000 or so, I wouldn't be too quick to jump at the chance to work for them. POKER DON"T KISS NO ASS, AND POKER AIN'T NO YES MAN (now you offer me six figures, I'll say yes to everything in 3 languages.) But that's probably why I don't get asked to do a lot of shows with the "30 boys". I'm not in the A-crowd. To hell with them as long as I got My-crowd.

Until next time, take care, and keep your pimp hand strong.

## MARCH PHOTOS

Center middle clockwise: Alan Steele receiving award from Brian Tramel, Jason Reed [photo by Rick Nelson – Printmaster Photography], Billy Russ, Pappy/Brian Tramel, "Midnight Gold" [Greg Anthony/Brian Thompson/Bobby Eaton] with awards, Bolivar poster and D-Rock with "Good Call" and "Bad Call" poses.

## APRIL

**-Arena Report: RCW Trumann, AR 4.02.10**

----Christian Jacobs beat Bishop…Jon Michael beat Ron Rage…Rodney Mack beat Seth Knight
 ….Stan Lee beat Greg Anthony. [***3/4] …"Midnight Gold" [Greg Anthony/Bobby Eaton] beat "High Stakes" [Chris O'Neal/Stan Lee].

Full Report and notes go to: *Yearbook 2010 Web Companion-*

**-Pokerface wins MCW Title for the first time Oseola, AR 4.02.10.**

**-Arena Report: ASWF Tuckerman, AR 4.03.10**

----Little Devil vs Kid J – No contest…Dante Cain/Hot Rod Ellison beat Kevin Charles/The Enforcer…Seth Sabor beat Eric Wayne…Johnny Hawk beat X-Kalibur…Wild Bill beat Kid Nikels. Nikels…Cason McCain & "Big Rig" Cody Murdoch with Athena Eclipse beat Christopher Lee/Lee Michaels….Austin Lane beat Mike Anthony [***3/4]…Casino Kid/Kid J beat Little Devil/Demon X.

Full Report and notes go to: *Yearbook 2010 Web Companion-*

**-NEW Leaves ASWF.**

----Eric Wayne, Kid Nikels, Dan Matthews and Kevin Charles are gone from ASWF. The reason given "officially" is they are citing a disagreement with the office. I am hearing "off the record" of it being money problems and also it will soon become a conflict of interest. NEW staff will be pushed RIGHT on upcoming RCW shows [including TV]. This might be the first move of "drawing a line in the sand" of who works for whom between ASWF/RCW.

 ----A few things to look at and wonder also. Where will Mike Anthony end up?? Will he stay with both promotions or only NEW?? What will this mean to Casino Kid, who works for both promotions?? Will Austin Lane, who has been featured as a major player in NEW, still work for NEW?? RCW adding some of the NEW names will easily make it the best roster in this area EVER during the RRO era. The weak link of the whole crew would be Dan Matthews. Matthews is the top candidate for Rookie of the Year this year and had a better match with Alan Steele on RCW TV than 75% of the ASWF show. That just shows you the depth and strength of the RCW crew.

----Only time will tell whether a group like RCW, just doing the simple things like using the best talent, advertising, and putting on quality shows can draw. This group has everything going for it; hopefully it can be successful at the gate.

**-ASWF Strikes Back!**

*"This really has nothing to do with RCW. ASWF tried to get TV in different markets, but that was the only one they could find that was affordable. RCW has better talent and will have a better show. ASWF will present a show that is a commercial for people coming out to our weekly show in Tuckerman. They are not going to go to Trumann, Augusta or wherever."* **Austin Lane talking with RRO on Sunday morning.**

----At that point Lane didn't even know ASWF was booked for Augusta tonight. They didn't even plug it at the show Saturday night. The truth is – ASWF has made the next move in this battle. David Walls made the decision to run Augusta, AR [a town that RCW is trying to make a regular stop] on Tuesday of this week. Apparently posters did not go up until yesterday. They are trying to book a show a week before the RCW show. It was also hinted to me that this might have to do with the NEW guys leaving ASWF.

----I guess in this era of wrestling, all is fair; huh?? No one has territories. No one has integrity or loyalty towards one promotion or another?? The main objection I have to all of this is product confusion. If a wrestling fan goes to this ASWF show and they pay $6 for Demon X and Wild Bill, then when it comes to RCW they will think it is the same product. And believe me – it is not. RCW will give them guys like Greg Anthony and Stan Lee for a $10 ticket price and be worth it, but a casual fan will not see that.

----While David Walls is continuing to try to do things to interrupt RCW, RCW is "business as usual" full steam ahead just doing what they do. In this small war of sorts, you have a promotion like RCW that just started promoting that seems to be bothering Walls. Why would they bother him so much?? Isn't ASWF an established name that should just go on with their business?? As I always say, only time will tell. It will be fun to see how this all ends and it is easily the hottest story so far this year.

**-Southside Brawler beats Pokerface to win DCW Title Jonesboro, AR 4.03.10**

**-"Midnight Gold" beat "New Age Outlaws" – TGB pins Billy Gunn.**

----RRO Tag Team of the Year 2009 "Midnight Gold" [Bobby Eaton/Greg Anthony] with Brian Thompson beat "New Age Outlaws" [Billy Gunn/Jesse James] last night [Saturday] in Fort Smith, AR. Greg Anthony pinned Gunn using a gimmick for the win. The two teams worked each other the night before in Springdale, AR with "Outlaws" winning. I should have full results sometime later in the week.

**-Arena Report: MCW Osceola, AR 4.10.10**

----Homer Lee/Canadian Phoenix beat Pedro Hambone/BlackJack…C-Money by DQ over Ray…Big Daddy LaFonce/Frankie Tucker beat Adrian Stratton/Kilo…V-Man/Officer Hudson beat Aaron Ecstasy/C-Money…Pokerface beat Bishop with special ref Big Jim in a Ghetto Street fight. [***3/4]

Full Report and notes go to: *Yearbook 2010 Web Companion-*

**-The Golden Circle: "Metro Sexual Mania?" by Greg Anthony**

Wrestling is a tough business. We've got grown men throwing and slamming each other and, contrary to popular belief, it hurts. In addition, we've all got that "jock" mentality. Machismo reaching a boiling point a lot of times. With all that being said, Metro sexual Mania is still running wild in pro wrestling.

Here I am in a locker room with some of the toughest men I've ever known and I hear things like... "Do I look bloated?", "Your abs look great", "Does my ass look flat in these tights?". Everyone has said or done something to that extent. Have you ever asked another man to rub baby oil on your back? Not acceptable at the gym but it's ok in pro wrestling. Some of the things I've seen and heard would make a great Saturday Night Live skit.

We all have friends outside the business. Being in Tennessee some of mine are good ole boys from the country. Things that are musts/requirements in wrestling seem very gay to the average male. Like highlighting your hair or the extensive man-scaping that goes on with a pro wrestler. Even tanning in a tanning bed is a little much for some men.

Once, back in the LAW in Dyersburg days, Christian Jacobs had a run-in during the show. So CJ was dressed in a pair of jeans with no shirt and had oiled up. Waiting for his spot, Chris O'Neal comes and asks if he has time to run to Taco Bell with him? CJ agrees and hops in the car with Chris. They get back and tell me they went to the drive thru. I can only imagine what the people working the window must have been thinking with two males, one shirtless and oiled up coming thru. The best part is that Chris was wearing a Picture Perfect t-shirt with his and CJ's picture on the front. You can't write stuff like that.

Is metro sexuality good or bad for wrestling? I can't answer that myself. I think we are more a product of the environment than anything else. We are constantly under the microscope like super models. To be thin, tan or whatever magazine dream people think we should be, thus creating this sometime insecurity about our appearance. I say be healthy but be you, I promise you can't go wrong with that. And when "The Golden Boy' Greg Anthony makes a promise, it's as good as gold.

**-Wayne's World: "Life of a Wrestler" by Eric Wayne.**

From the everyday aches and pains, to the sacrifices that are made…the life of a wrestler is definitely an adventure til the end. Not much of it makes sense at times, but not everything has to make sense. It all adds up over time and in the end, all that matters is being inside the ring. It's an incredible sensation to make the fans scream, cheer, boo, cry, or go completely and eerily silent, watching people throw whatever is available or physically being held back by security. What's equally as important as that is the challenge of making a living in a business that has gone downhill tremendously when compared to what it once was. For those with the heart and dedication to become the best, it's a long road but the final destination is worth the trip. The normal person never seems to quite understand why anyone would put themselves through so much for what seems like so little. It's always hard to explain because the answer changes all the time, for me at least.

The aches and pains that we feel everyday are what people in their 40's and 50's are supposed to feel, not someone in their mid-20's. It's not much different than what any other athlete feels on any given day, but the injuries seem to happen more often. It's rarely anything major but whether it's jumping from 10 feet in the air or being hit with chairs…or something as simple as a bodyslam or clothesline, it all adds up over time.

The sacrifices made aren't always physical either. It doesn't make sense to normal people that we would drive 3 hours for a 5 second match, which I did for several weeks. But the fact that we sometimes have to be gone all day for a 20 minute match at night can be confusing. Missing birthdays, funerals, weddings and countless other events are all just part of the life of a wrestler. When it comes to a wrestling family, you can count on a few of us being late or not there at all because of previous obligations. Making it home at 2 in the morning only to have to wake up at 7am is a normal occurrence for us as well.

The only thing people ever see is the final product. What happens in the ring is only 10% of what happens in the life of a wrestler. Long hours on the road, dealing with nagging injuries, missing time with family and friends, training to stay well conditioned…it's all part of a normal day for us. It's not much different than what any other athlete goes through, but the life of a wrestler can be just as strenuous as the life of any other athlete. Most of the time though, we face conditions that normal athletes don't. A lot of the time we deal with other wrestlers with a serious lack of training, poor building conditions, low pay and lots of bumps, bruises, and soreness. But most of us have the same dream: a full time job wrestling. Once we fulfill our dream, nothing else matters.

**- CWA draws 500-650 in return to Ripley, MS 4.24.10.** [Go to *Yearbook 2010 Web Companion* for full results]

**-Coach's Corner "I Watched More Than 60 Seconds of RCW TV" by Brian Tramel**

---I have been fortunate enough to be able to join RCW for two of their TV tapings and recently sat down to watch all of the TV shows that have aired up to this point. Is the show good?? Yes, it reminds me of the old TV show that used to air [ a lot like Continental] and it features some of the best local talent in the area. If you have not had the chance to watch the show, then take a few minutes out [30 to be exact] every week to sit down and enjoy a really fun wrestling TV show. I have seen a few mistakes and will make note of them below, but this is minor stuff. The quality of the show is better than anything that has aired so far this year [I had to quit IWA after the infamous "music" show]. As I have seen on various websites before, this is my opinion and mine alone, but it is coming from a guy that sat down and watched all the shows, not from someone that tried to form an opinion by watching just "60 seconds.

GOOD

-Seth Knight has been a total trooper for this show.  His three TV bouts have been some of the best TV bouts in a while.  First against Christian Jacobs, then a great match against Justin Smart and then a good interview followed by him putting over Rodney Mack like a million bucks.  Smart has also improved tons working for NEW in a TV setting and really shined in that bout.

-Bobby Eaton is put in the perfect position here – whether he is teaming with Greg Anthony or receiving the key to the city, this is the kind of role you would want a "legend" to have.

-Matt Riviera is a star.  The viginette that aired along with his angle against Ron Rage – all top notch.  His interview with the dog food – "Bacon!! Bacon!!" was just so bizarre and funny – it was off the charts.  That interview would have been something that in the 1980's would have inspired all my friends and I to go around school yelling "Bacon!! Bacon!!" at each other.

-Casino Kid is in the perfect role here also.  Not too much wrestling – a lot of talking.

-"The Golden Boy" Greg Anthony is one of the best talkers...or maybe THE best talker…in the area.  Great skills.

-Brian Thompson takes the time to get over all the angles.  Rodney Mack walks out and Thompson puts him over like a true star.  Thompson also [even though he is trying to get over that SO MUCH is happening] doesn't give you too much to digest.

-"Premiere Brutality" [Eric Wayne/Kid Nikels] looked really good as a team.  Please give Kid more mic time!!  His stuff is so fun!!

-Check out the intensity of Rodney Mack!!  He comes off with just an edge above the pack.  Just think – Mack, Riviera and Worthington as a heel trio??

-The build for a Jon Michael Worthington vs Christian Jacobs RCW Title Tournament Final – could there be a better final??

BAD

-The mic needed to be plugged to the camera for the Casino/TGB angle.  Hard to hear everything.

-You could see the top of the backdrop on some of the interviews.

-Thompson cut himself off before one of matches.

www.rasslinriotonline.com

-Riviera and Worthington have almost the same gimmick, but that will probably put them together.

-You could see empty chairs.

-Thompson talked about speaking with Ron Rage before the match, but they should have aired an actual interview with him.

-Two camera video shoot!!

----I was being a bit picky on some of my BAD comments, but it is just a few things that would take this from being a good TV show to a GREAT TV show.  If you are a wrestling fan in this area, do yourself a favor – search the archives or go to http://www.rcwwrestling.com/ and check out all the shows up to this point.

APRIL PHOTOS

Left to right top: Pokerface and JD Kerry with 2009 Award

Left to right bottom: Jazz with 2009 Award and Ken Wayne/Jason Reed

**MAY**

**-The Thompson Perspective by Brian Thompson**

It has been a very, very long time since I sat down and penned an edition of "The Thompson Perspective" for RasslinRiotOnline. I won't waste a lot of time with the opening paragraph of this particular column. I'll just get right down to business.

As I look at the calendar, I rapidly see a "wrestling anniversary" approaching for me. In a matter of days, 14 to be exact, I will celebrate my 10-year anniversary in the wrestling business. My how time certainly does get away from us!

Ten years ago, I was given the opportunity to get into the wrestling business by Ben Oliver, who wrestled professionally as "Big Bad Ben" and to all of the boys was known as "Triple B." I still have the old e-mail he sent me giving me the chance to start this 10-year rollercoaster ride. Here it is:

*"Brian,*

*It's time to step up to the plate. I'd asked if you ever had thought about being a ring announcer. Well if you are still interested we have a slot open May 20th. Call me today 314 XXX XXXX.*

*BBB"*

Obviously the "X's" indicate a phone number that he had at the time. I remember all this like it were yesterday.

Ben's company was Gateway Championship Wrestling, based in St. Louis, MO. He started it just months after its predecessor Midwest Renegade Wrestling went out of business. GCW was a quality independent promotion.

In the previous 12 months, I had gotten my foot in the door at MRW by doing website reports and show recaps. When GCW formed, I started doing the same for them. It was a huge moment being able to go backstage at GCW's first show. Today, it seems that everything is so open that I really wonder if it is as meaningful to break in as it used to be.

Anyway, I'm not going to rant and rave. There is plenty of that stuff out all over the internet.

I'm sitting here right now, reflecting on my career. It has been an interesting ride to say the least.

If I review my financial standing, based on my wrestling career, I can't say that it has been a success. But if I measure the other things of more sentimental value – friendships, being able to perform in front of fans, meeting other people, getting to travel the country, etc. – then it HAS been a success.

Two of my favorite phrases when talking to friends such as Brian Tramel and "Golden Boy" Greg Anthony are "Let me tell you what is wrong with the wrestling business" and "Don't talk to me today, I hate the wrestling business."

Well, as frustrated as I can get, I still have to reflect fondly on the past 10 years and say that I have been truly blessed.

Let me tell you a true story that will, especially if you are in the business, make you feel pride in knowing what you are a part of.

When I was putting the initial plans for Ringside Championship Wrestling (RCW) together, I was looking at the Wynne, AR market. Jamie Jay and his PWA promotion had run a few shows in Wynne off and on, but I wasn't sure if he intended to continue to do so or not. Anyway, I was in talks with a young man in Wynne about getting involved in the promotion.

It was his lifelong dream to be in the wrestling business. He was just 15, so actual in-ring competition was still far away, but as a student still in school he could be a great asset to help promote the new company. He was also a student who was taught by my wife during her recent internship.

This young man was very excited about the thought that in 2010, he would be involved with the wrestling business. Everytime I logged onto Facebook when he was also logged on, inevitably within 30 seconds I had a chat window pop up and he just couldn't wait to talk about wrestling, RCW and everything. So we chatted. He had the usual exciting questions of, "Can I manage, can I do this or can I do that?" Of course, I had to slow him down and tell him that those things take time.

I was looking forward to having him on staff as a helper when we debuted.

I saw him around the first of December during the annual Wynne Christmas Parade, which is put together by the Cross County Chamber of Commerce where I work my regular job. He was excited to see me and to win the "Grand Champion" float prize for the work of the local boy scout troup he was involved with.

Around Christmas time, I stopped hearing from him. I didn't think anything about it. My daily life was busy with work, family and getting RCW off the ground. Our first show was cancelled, then rescheduled and finally happened. Ironically, after all the build-up for it, I hadn't heard a peep from this young man. I did know he had talked to Jamie too about helping with PWA, which was now planning to run Vanndale, AR, just five miles north of Wynne. I actually assumed that he got involved with PWA and was too busy to juggle helping both groups.

The other day, his face popped up on Facebook in the section that tells you to "Reconnect" with someone. So I clicked on his page. I began reading messages from people saying they missed him. At first I'm thinking, he just moved away. As I read more messages, it became more apparent that moving wasn't the case. This 15-year-old young man had died in early January.

To say I was stunned would be an understatement. As I read more messages, specifically those from around his death, I discovered that he had had several major surgeries on his heart when he was just 18 months old. I had no clue.

Then, reading a post by his father, I learned that he was granted a wish by the "Make-A-Wish Foundation" to go to WrestleMania 26 this year, but he didn't live to see that chance.

Shame on me for ever really whining about this business. Shame on me for complaining about making a trip. Shame on me for not always remembering what an honor it is to be a part of professional wrestling.

At least I got my chance 10 years ago and the dream continues to this day. This youngster didn't make it that far.

(Brian Thompson is the co-owner, booker and announcer for Ringside Championship Wrestling. He may be reached by e-mail at bptbookings@yahoo.com)

**-HCW draws 400+ in Jackson, TN 5.07.10 with Kevin White vs Brian Christopher main event. Go to _Yearbook 2010 Web Companion_ for full results.**

**-New Memphis Wrestling TV tapings announced to be taped at The Vine in Midtown Memphs.**

**-The Straight Flush by Pokerface.**

Sacrifices

Not sure if I have talked about this before, but it will not hurt to touch on it again. To be a success at anything, sacrifices have to made. Some small, then more times than not, some great. That's just life. If you're not willing to make those sacrifices, you aren't ready to reap the rewards.

In this business that I have chosen, I have given up some things. Nothing that can't be replaced. Honestly, if I could go back I really don't think I would change a thing. Well, except, maybe having my wrist broken. We often sacrifice time, effort, personal pleasures, and at times emotional peace of mind. But it's a necessary evil. I don't think we, at least on the independent level, have it as hard as wrestlers of yesteryear. But it can still be difficult nonetheless. It's emotionally draining to scratch and claw to get to the next level, and doors are constantly being shut in your face. It's frustrating to drive to a match to perform and make it back home with less in your pocket than what you started with. But that's the life that we've chosen. From personal experience, it's upsetting to be constantly told that you are too small, yet a guy who is the same size or smaller gets a job.

A lot of us truly dedicated wrestlers, for the most part, don't have a personal life. Some of us work a job all week, and wrestle on the weekend. Therefore, "me" time is obsolete. We make sacrifices with our body. Over time, most of us move around like we are 20 years older than we really are. Some of us may feel the need to resort to drugs for various reasons, which also has the potential of taking its toll on us physically. Some of us sacrifice starting a family. To a certain point, I can attest to that. Well, I've yet to get married. Mainly because I feel it would hinder me. Some of our families have had to suffer because of our relationship with this business. So not only do we sacrifice, but our loved ones also. The family I did have up until last year, I don't feel they really suffered. For years a lot of the times they would be with me on the road. So I can't blame it on the wrestling.

Like I said earlier, some sacrifices have to made. You can't really enjoy the good times, if you don't know how to deal with the bad times. The sacrifices can help mold us into better, more appreciative performers. We can't have everything given to us on a silver platter. Sometimes you're going to have it handed to you wrapped in s**t, covered with mud, with a side of maggots. We at times have to sacrifice our pride. We get talked down to, get made fun of, ignored, taken for granted, overworked, underpaid, overlooked, and under appreciated. But like anything in life, once you've fought the war, victory is sooooooooooo sweet.

Until next time, keep your pimp hand strong.

**-Mama Says It Bees That Way Sometimes "Pet Peeves" by Downtown Bruno**

Hello cyber friends!! Sorry it's been so long since my last post, but between my job at WWE and NEW responsibilities, and having to take care of my home responsibilities [cutting grass, laundry, maintenance] – there's not much time left over. But, since I've got a few minutes to spare here, I thought I would pass on some of my pet peeves. You will either give me a nod of agreement or there will be some awkward acknowledgements from those people who behave this way.

When WWE comes to Memphis, don't automatically assume that just because I work for the WWE and may know you, that this entitles you to free tickets. It doesn't work that way. First of all, we make our living by selling tickets, ppvs, etc. If we give it away, then we do not make a living. Make sense?? Yes, I do receive a few comp tickets that I give to family and close friends, but not that many. Could I come to your job and get free food/car repair/haircuts/healthcare ???

Also, those that come up to me with the annoying bulls**t of saying they would like to get them tickets, but they don't mind paying for them are 100% full of S**T!! And you know who YOU are! If you don't mind paying for them, why the hell are you coming to me?? I am not Ticketmaster!! Why?? Because you think I will say, "No...No...let me give you free ones!!" I am not stupid. That's why you came to me in the first place!!

Also, NO you cannot come in the back and meet the wrestlers, meet Vince McMahon, have your picture taken with the Divas, etc. It's a place of business where a multi-million dollar weekly TV show is being produced – not play time for you and your kids.

I could go on and on for hours about stupid questions I hear on a regular basis!

*"Half that wrestling is fake!"*

Which half?? That's my question??

*"I saw two guys who just beat the s\*\*t out of each other out drinking together after the show."*

This is too stupid to even warrant a response! After the show, we move on to the next town, go home or whatever. We don't have time to go and socialize for the next part. I have been hearing this for 30 f'n years! Variations of it have included Lawler and Dundee [even though they were not hang out buddies anyway and Lawler never drank in his life], Sputnik and Billy Wicks, etc...BULLS\*\*T!!

What else?? Let's see…No, I can't get you autographs!! I am too busy and so are the WWE superstars. It's not something that I want to get a reputation for being a pain in the ass. NO!! I can not get you t-shirts, dvds, video games, hats, action figures and those of you lying %#&\*#^#^ that say you don't mind paying for items...then...WHY ASK ME?? Shop Zone – Concession Table!! Whatever...not me, just grow up. Thank you and good day to all.

**-RRO celebrates 4 years of the site. Brian Tramel steps down as editor in chief for a break and Gene Jackson takes over.**

**-Way Cool beats Kilo to win TIWF Title Trenton, TN 5.15.10**

**-Su Yung signs developmental deal with WWE.**

**-EWE closes their doors in Ripley, TN.**

**-ASWF draws 400+ for "Payback" with Demon X vs Jerry Lawler main event. Go to** *Yearbook 2010 Web Companion* **for full results.**

**-The Golden Circle: "All Hail The Overlord" by Greg Anthony**

Wrestling is a business where proximity plays a big part. During the territory days, when each had their own stars, someone who might be the biggest star in Memphis may as well be named Joe Blow when he went to Portland. The same goes for our goals. If you grew up in Atlanta, then being a part of the NWA was always something you wanted to achieve. But if you grew up here, then being a part of Memphis Wrestling was your dream, more so than any other territory branded local TV show.  Because it was what you grew up on, and now you would have an opportunity to shine.  Sometimes things don't go as planned.

Memphis had two top notch federations in the early 2000s, Power Pro Wrestling and WWF(E) developmental Memphis Championship Wrestling.  When WWE pulled its developmental deal from MCW, MCW then joined with Power Pro.  However, it wasn't long before Power Pro itself became a thing of the past.  I was working for Sir Mo in Mid America Championship Wrestling at The Dyersburg Entertainment Center, when it was brought up that Jerry Lawler and crew was using DEC and most of MACW talent on what would be the next version of Memphis Wrestling.  It was a huge opportunity for us young guys.  Only a few years in the business and to be on such a program.

We taped every other Wednesday night and the show's time slot was 11am Saturday morning.  I remember being so excited after that first taping, like, "Wow, I'm going to be on Memphis Wrestlng!"  I was living by myself at the time and couldn't afford cable so I went over to my Grandma's house to watch the show that morning.  I was in a tag match with Bitty Little and was making myself a drink when Cory Maclin made the opening announcements.  I really wasn't paying attention and I heard him say "Bitty Little and ?????"  I didn't make out what he had said but I knew it didn't sound like Golden Boy.  So I watched the match and Bitty tagged me in and Corey said, "And here comes Overlord!!".  WTF!!  I'm sorry, did he just call me Overlord?  My heart sank.

I didn't know what to do or how to feel.  I mean, did he really think my name was Overlord?  Golden Boy – Overlord - yeah that rhymes.  Or was it a rib by someone on him, which really was a rib on me…or a rib on us both?  I soon got over it, big whoop, he called me the wrong name, but then I went to the show that night and the boys couldn't resist calling me Overlord ALL NIGHT LONG.  When something really bothers me, and I've run out of witty comebacks.  I usually repeat "F**k you" over and over.

It's just one of those funny little stories, when the business provides a little comic relief.  Worse things could have happened, like they really wanted me to be called Overlord, like when they wanted to call Flair Spartacus.  I made it out of that night alive and with my sanity.  Just remember you never know what's lurking in the shadows or in Cory Maclin's commentary….All Hail Overlord!!!

**-Arena Report: NBW "Spring Breakout 2010" Newbern, TN 5.29.10**

----Blaine Devine beat Oz …Hardcore Yow won the NBW High Risk title in a 5-way…
Sarge O'Reilly beat Shannon Lee…Eric Wayne over Brad Badd and Mark Justice in a 3-way…
Cody Melton/Derrick King beat Kid Nikels/Jason Reed to win the NBW Tag Team titles…
Chris Rocker beat Jeremy Moore by submission to win the NBW Title…Jay Lethal beat Matt Riviera.

Full Report and notes go to:  *Yearbook 2010 Web Companion.*

## MAY PHOTOS

Middle: Su Yung Left branch: Chris Rocker, Frank Martin and Demon X with"Hollywood" Jimmy
Right branch: Maxx Corbin, Cody Melton/Derrick King celebrating 4 Years of RRO and XOW
poster.

JUNE

-**Memphis Wrestling returns to local TV.**

-**Tatt2 wears tape on this hands and is asked to leave NEW dressing room.**

-**DCW closes their doors in Jonesboro, AR.**

----I am hearing from various sources that DCW in Jonesboro, AR either had their final show last night or they are within a few weeks of shutting down. In January 2008, RWA debuted with about 200 people in attendance at the main event with Jerry Lawler vs Reno Diamond in the King Sportatorium, which later became the Dogg House. In August last year, there was a much publicized split of RWA owner Frank Martin and Rodney Mack, which would bring about the name change and new direction of the company. [*Yearbook 2009*] Many insiders felt that the promotion never regained steam lost from that split, even though the booking seemed to be good. Mack changed the name of the promotion to DCW, changed the ticket prices, and everytime I was there, they put on a quality show. DCW placed in the Promotion of the Year 2009 voting. Rodney Mack also finished as one of the top four wrestlers in this area and in the top 3 in Wrestler of the Year voting, losing only by 7 points.

----Late last month, EWE shut the doors. EWE was considered a staple of this area. The promotion opened the doors as TLCW and won RRO Promotion of the Year 2006 and 2007. They also took Booker of the Year honors both years and Arena Report Match of the Year in 2007. Derrick King, who was featured as the main star in 2006 and 2007, won Wrestler of the Year honors in both years.

----Two promotions dead before half of 2010 is over is not a good sign. RCW and Jerry Lawler's Memphis Wrestling have added their names to the hat and will give guys a different place to work. The bad thing about promotions closing is that the boys will have fewer places to work, but in turn, the promoters may benefit from the level of talent being better.

-**The "Asylum" [Pappy/Psycho] beat NSFC [Izzy Rotten/Brad Simpson] & "Hard Justice" [Big Bob/Lawman Williams] to win the TIWF Tag Team Titles. 6.05.10**

-**The Royal Flush – Pokerface Talks About DCW**

I know I haven't posted a column lately due to personal issues, but I felt a need to speak up.

It's no secret that DCW has ended. I have received numerous texts asking me about the situation. Honestly, some things I have no idea about. I've heard pretty much the same stories most of you have. Well, here's my take on DCW from beginning to end.

First, I will start with RWA, DCW's old name. We shut down due to management conflict. I will say it was one of, if not my favorite, Indy show to be a part of. One of my biggest gripes about it was that the owner needed to let the booker book. By the way that had nothing to do with the company ending, but I felt the need to say it. I had/have no issues with the former owner. I didn't like some things that he did, but that's just business. Anyway, after the demise of RWA, I truly did feel a loss, until I got a call from Rodney saying we would be up and running again in mid September '09. GREAT!

When we re-opened, the show had a different feel. Not better or worse, just different. I was happy to see and work with my co-wrestlers once again, and everybody seemed happy to see each other. We had even brought in two big names in the biz, Sid Vicious and Scott Hall. I had the privilege to work with them both. It also gave us a chance to ask them questions and what-not. We've always had a somewhat tight knit locker room. We had one boss. Again, ONE, boss. The owner let Rodney do his job with, to my knowledge, no interference. That, in return, made things run a lot smoother. It's true we weren't packing the house, but it had nothing to do with the quality of the show. It was just one of those things. RWA crowds, before the demise, had started to drop some also.

Around November '09, Rodney, here and there, had started getting out of town bookings. So you can say I was kind of in charge. I couldn't really enjoy myself or the show at first because I was such a detail freak. At first Rodney booked the matches, and would relay them to me. Then little by little, I would have almost 100% creative control, with final approval from Rodney. As time went on, I got more relaxed with my position. I will go on record to say that I did not run the show alone. I had help and sought advice from the other talent. If I couldn't figure something out, I had no problem asking for help, or they would just come to me. So it was a team effort. Guys like the Blazer, S. Brawler, L. Northern, R. Little, and the Violent Mexican helped out a lot. ( I kinda didn't wanna give their wrestling names, lol) After every show, I would call and give Mack a report. I tried to involve everybody in the show from the trainees, to the girls, to the vets. Unlike some people who book, I didn't make it the Pokerface show. I did, however, at times get more time in matches and segments because I was the champion. That, in return, would emphasize the importance of the power and privilege of the title, not to get me over.

Rodney wanted to give DCW, the original ECW feel, where everybody chipped in and we were like a family. I can honestly say we were. Saturdays couldn't come fast enough for me. We would train around one o'clock until about 4 pm, go have lunch, and come back for the show. Everybody tried to make everybody better. We would have a few drinks, socialize, and shoot the breeze with each other. But it was always business first. At one time Rodney felt that the rookies were partying too much and their performance was lacking, so he forbade them to have a drink until they got with it. Two rookies seemed to have an attitude problem, so he made them train, but they couldn't do the show. I would at times during the pre-show meeting voice certain rules, and some guys would get pissed. But I told them that whatever rules I laid out were first approved by Rodney, so go see him if you don't like it.

Over the last couple of months everybody stepped up so much that it made Mack's job easier. We had different guys come in from Louisiana and Texas to work. It was great. The crowds just weren't coming in. The tickets prices were raised. I'm assuming that was to keep the rent paid and the lights on. Not to mention pay us. We did lose a few guys due to certain issues, from money to people being an ass to them. I have played advocate for a lot of the guys. Many guys were on the chopping block or were actually "fired", and I spoke up and pleaded their case for business' sake. Many, to this day, still don't know who they are.

Now Saturday, June 5, 2010. The day everybody wants to know about. First I would like to say that part of me had a feeling that DCW in that building was nearing an end. That was just from me observing the low crowds and having an idea what the rent was. Anyway, before I left for the show that afternoon, someone had texted me asking was that night going to be the last show. I truly hadn't heard anything. Fast Forward. That day I came back from lunch in Jonesboro, and I saw the owner of the building putting up a For Lease sign. I'm like WTF! So then I hear that the show was canceled. So I was told to call the guys who were coming in that night from Dyersburg, and tell them not to come. I admit I was sad. Rodney was cool, but seemed bothered. I was in the locker room maybe an hour later, drinking beer cocktails, when I was told the show was back on. So we ran the show with the "originals" so to speak. So it was an emotional night to say the least. After Southside defeated me in my final shot at the DCW title in that building, he cried. J.D. Kerry wept because that was the building he started in. Everybody was showing much love afterwards. As for the building being destroyed, I can say some doors were torn down. But most of the damage that was done, was done to the things that the promoter put his money in. Things that weren't there before. We always worked real rough, wrestled real rough. It's on film that just about every week there was this wall that separated the fans from our dressing room that we tried to put a hole in by throwing each other into it. There is this table we had been trying to break for 2 years. We had almost broke the garage door to the building a few months back. If it got out of hand, it was because ALL the wrestlers were sad. Tejano Kid would drive 9 hours from Texas every week to be there. It wasn't for the money. Me and some of the other guys could've been doing shows elsewhere for a little more money, but we chose to stay at DCW.

DCW was the first company I have ever worked for to let me completely use my ideas. It let me truly be Pokerface. As far as the rent not being paid or trouble with the Athletic Commission, I've only heard hearsay. Honestly, in depth things about the bills and other things, Rodney never shared that with me, and it wasn't my place to know anyway. I will say this, things may or may not have got of hand at the show, but I can say, we, DCW, went out with a bang! Until next time, God bless you, and keep your pimp hand strong.

**-Brian Tramel returns to helm of RRO after 3 week break.**

**-Dustin Starr featured on www.fcwwrestling.com**

 ----As many of you know, Dustin Starr reported to work for the WWE developmental territory in mid-March. Starr is known now in the WWE Universe as Daniel Skyler [at least he kept his initials]. Skyler is working as a WWE ref.

----Skyler has reffed matches featuring all NXT guys as well as main events on FCW TV. He also worked the Smackdown and NXT tapings that were in Tampa last week. He is currently writing for the FCW magazine and his "Kickout" brand of shirts are being sold at www.fcwwrestling.com. You can follow Skyler now on Twitter - DanielSkyler.

----RRO would like to extend our best wishes to Skyler, and let him know the whole staff and his friends back here in the RRO Universe are very proud of him and his accomplishments. The WWE got a "good hand" with Skyler and we look forward to following him on his journey.

**-TCW draws 300 in Pine Bluff, AR with Lethal Romance (Matt Riviera & Jay Lethal) vs Tag Team Champions The Dark Circle (Tim Storm & Apoc) 6.12. Go to *Yearbook 2010 Web Companion* for full results.**

**-Randy Hales returns to Memphis Wrestling.**

----There are just some random notes from the tapings below, but it looks like the big news coming out of the taping is that **Randy Hales has returned to wrestling**. The sources that I talked to said that Hales was involved in helping run the show. Not sure what his "official" capacity is or will be, but he is involved in the show. Hales became a favorite of this site when he joined Gene Jackson for three episodes of *Cheap Heat Radio* scoring over 4000 downloads for his shows in his first interview since 2001. Hales made his return to wrestling in April 2008 for a two show stint at TLCW in Ripley, TN. Hales also was involved in the 2008 and 2009 *4th in the Forest* shows in an angle with Brandon Baxter, which actually started on the third episode of CHR that he recorded.

----All I can say is "wow!" This has the potential to be one of the best wrestling shows in this area in a long time. You have guys like Hales, Baxter, King, Wayne, Lawler and Bert Prentice all under one roof!! They are also featuring some of the best talent in the area along with some of the best wrestling minds. At least they got me to wanting to watch the show.

**-Demon X and Wild Bill beat Morgan Williams/X-Kaliber to win ASWF Tag Team Titles Tuckerman, AR 6.12.10**

**-Jon Michael Worthington beat Christian Jacobs to win RCW Title Tournament Final Forrest City, AR 6.19.10. Go to *Yearbook 2010 Web Companion* for full results.**

**-Coach's Corner "Going into Business for Yourself" by Brian Tramel.**

Is it ok to go in business for yourself when it comes to working for a local promotion?? If you are not familiar with the term, then it can best be described as not following the storyline lined out by the booker and doing something that will get you over more. At times it might just be a way for you to get back at the promoter. There have been some famous incidents, including one of my most memorable ones as a fan – Akira Madea shoot kicked Riki Choshu in the face as Choshu had a scorpion leglock on his opponent. This incident would totally change Japanese wrestling as

Madea became a huge star because everyone thought he was REAL. The infamous Bret Hart-Vince McMahon incident may be considered a bit of "going in business for yourself", but in reality Vince was just going to business for his business. Madusa pitched the WWE Ladies title in the trash on WCW. That really helped her career, didn't it??

I went in business for myself one time. And, after all these years, I would probably do it again, but in hindsight – it was not the right thing to do. Brickhouse Brown was on a local show on Sunday afternoon for MSWA. I was able to see his payoff along with that of another guy he brought with him. Both guys got paid $50 or more. I was highly pissed. My crew of five guys would be lucky to take home $25 for all of us. I was pissed and it was the last straw in a long list of bad payoffs. I went to the babyfaces and told them to forget the finish; we had a new finish. We would enter the ring – chokeslam someone and pin him – we go home. The thing I did not tell the faces was that I was also going to get on the mic and say that if my team lost, then my whole team would leave MSWA. It was a 10-man tag [if I can remember right] and we all packed our bags before the match started. I did the mic spill, they entered the ring – 3 count and we walked out the side door to go home.

Did I accomplish anything? Nah. Did it help my guys? No. Was it Brickhouse Brown's fault?? No, it wasn't. Brown is a freakin' legend and whatever he asked to be paid – he deserved it and honestly it was NONE OF MY BUSINESS.

So, you might be saying to yourself, "Coach is telling us he did it, but don't do it." Yes I am. It falls in that category with "do what I say, not what I did." If a promoter hires a booker for a promotion and puts his faith in that guy to run the show, then it is not ok to go against the booker's plan, even if you are the promoter. You got one guy spending all his free time trying to book a show and the promoter changes everything five minutes before the show starts. Or, on the other hand, you got a promoter that [with help from the encouragement of a worker] decides it is ok to change an angle right in the middle of the show. Believe me – the promoter should stay away from the ring on most incidents unless your name is Ken Wayne or Jerry Lawler. If you think it is ok to go into business for yourself, then you know NOTHING about the business. If you don't like the booker, then walk out the door. If you don't like the direction you are going in, give your notice. Anything you will do to ONLY put yourself over will not do anything to help the promotion as a whole.

**-MACW gets a new booker.**

----Ok, so here is a group that has had a fair share of people booking them, walking out on them, and low crowds. In February 2009 with Derrick King as booker, this show was packing close to 200 in the building for about a month. Crowds were good, and then it all started falling apart. King was replaced as booker, Chris Rocker took over the job, then later in the year became the "owner" and then later in the year left. They went through a name change from DCW to MACW, and they recently started booking shows on Saturday nights head to head with NBW. [And, remember, NBW was forced out of the Jukebox Café/Country Nights arena in November, 2008 by building owners Dale and Sandra Walker after a family dispute.] As of two weeks ago, they still are not drawing well – in the 50 range.

----The booker has switched hands almost every month this year. It started with Brian Steele and Tim Edwards, then Edwards/Jon Michael, then Edwards/Steele, then Edwards/Allen Walker. I think I got that straight. LOL Tim Edwards [who is family to the Walkers] then walks out and is gone. Your OWN family is quitting on you!!

----It now brings you to this past Saturday night, as Derrick King with booking help from Jason Reed, Stan Lee and Cody Melton will now run shows on Saturday at the Jukebox Café. Chris O'Neal is also on the roster and helping out. The big question is – will it matter?? Can these guys bring back the crowd?? I know they all would love to get that Dyersburg Entertainment Center crowd back, but have the fans been burned too much in that building?? Or are the fans just tired of the same old guys?? And can they out draw NBW, which is only 5 miles away, with limited or no advertising?? After all the dust has cleared during these battles of bookers and ownership, NBW has remained the only constant thing in the Dyersburg area. Will it continue to be that way??

## JUNE PHTOOS

**Top row left to right: Antwane Wise, Johnny Hawk and Kevin White**

**Bottom left to right: Tommy Mercer, Brian Christpoher and Jocephus**

# JULY

**-MACW gets a new owner.**

----In a move right out of a wrestling storyline, Jeremy Moore stepped into the MACW Dyersburg, TN arena Saturday night during the start of the opening match to announce that he is now the owner and operator of MACW. He let everyone know that he owned the promotion, telling them the new changes that were going to happen, including stripping Jon Michael of the MACW Title and the tag champs. He made himself the new MACW champion. He fired everyone on the MACW roster including Derrick King, Cody Melton, Jason Reed, Chris O'Neal and Stan Lee. [Moore kept only Tim Edwards and Gaylon Ray from the old crew] He made four matches for the night. After the 4th match, he told all the fans that they could go over to the NBW building and watch the rest of that show for FREE.

----At the NBW building, it was announced that Jeremy Moore and "Anarchy" members [Kevin Charles, Triple-C, Kid Nikels, Blaine Devine and Brian Badd] would not be attending the show that night. They set up a new main event of Chris Rocker vs Eric Wayne. During the main event [after the MACW fans had piled into the NBW arena], "Anarchy" came thru the front door and side door demolishing everyone in the NBW dressing room leaving them bloody in the ring. Moore even draped the MACW banner over the NBW crew.

----I should have the full rundown on both cards before the end of the week, but the story behind all of this is – Jeremy Moore did buy MACW. He bought all their equipment and now is the owner and operator of that promotion along with promoting in the Jukebox café building. He coordinated with Chris Rocker at the NBW building, so they presented two shows at the same time. RRO has covered the whole drama of this building and how Moore was asked to leave it when he started NBW. Derrick King, who just a few weeks back was named new booker for the third time in just a little over a year, is now out the door including his normal crew of guys. I don't know Moore's full plans, but this is the best way to eliminate your competition – buy them. I actually love the angle with Moore taking charge of MACW and it being the heel promotion and group. It makes for a great wrestling storyline with so much underlining shoot material that people will believe…well, because…most of it is true. Moore with this move has gone from me writing in 2007, "Is it good to have a teenage kid help book your show??" to Moore being the most powerful man in the Newbern/Dyersburg area.

**-Austin Lane beat Eric Wayne to win the US Jr Title 7.02.10 at NEW's "Stars & Stripes." Go to for ful results and notes:** *Yearbook 2010 Web Companion*

**-RCW folds after their final card at Craighead Forest Park in Jonesboro, AR for Fourth in the Forest Go to for ful results and notes:** *Yearbook 2010 Web Companion*

**-Stanley Clark passes away.**

----Stanley Clark, who wrestled in the 60's and 70's, passed away Tuesday morning. He was 68 years old - born in May, 1942. He also promoted shows in the area along with Don Bass. Ken Wayne met Clark's daughter Debbie when working for him, and she later became his wife. RRO would like to send our condolences and thoughts with Debbie and family.

**-The Golden Circle: "30" by Greg Anthony.**

Today's wrestlers aren't afraid of being paralyzed, the long term effects of steroids, or a half a dozen other reasonable things to be afraid of. The most terrifying thing for a pro wrestler in this era is the number 30. Or more specifically the age 30. The general consensus is that once you've hit the magic number, you've missed the boat. You may get good opportunities to work good shows, but the dream of being a WWE contracted wrestler is over. Is this fact or merely a bitter fiction that has made its bed in our world?

I did some heavy research for this article. I asked the question of several veterans who used to work the territories. Were they afraid of 30 or some other magical number? It wasn't that they were afraid of 30, but aware of it. If someone hadn't become a star or had gotten as good as they were going to by the time they hit 30, they usually started making alternative plans for the future. The big difference between then and now is that it was their decision. Plus, with several profitable companies and bookers, if one promoter didn't see anything in you, who's to say the next one wouldn't?

When Vince started offering contracts to guys to build a national WWF, He didn't hire guys 18-20 years old. He hired guys that were seasoned; guys that he knew could be in relatively any situation and they could perform, because this wouldn't be their first rodeo. And it made for a great product, where from top to bottom you had genuine workers. Guys that were working together to make money. Now everyone wasn't a Randy Savage or Ricky Steamboat, but everyone played their role perfectly.

Now it isn't to say that WWE has never and will never hire someone over the age of 30. Because they have, most notably guys like The Boogyman and Rico, who were in their late 30's even 40's when hired. The ratio to twenty-somethings vs thirty-plus is a one sided margin for sure. So what is "being in your prime" in pro wrestling now? You look at Shawn Michaels vs The Undertaker, two guys in their 40's who went and had probably the greatest match in Wrestlemania History. Neither man could have had that match when they were 25, because they hadn't had the 1000's of matches prior to learn from.

I personally know for a fact that if WWE would have hired me when I was 20 years old, I would have screwed it up in some way. Because I was stupid like all 20 year olds. It's like any sport, you draft someone directly out of high school and you have to deal with a maturing process. You draft a college senior and 4 year starter then, for the most part, you take that maturing process out of the equation. I personally would rather hire someone who is a great worker at 33, that could work for 10 more years, than someone who is gonna be just "ok" for 20. But I promise I don't know everything.


**-Mama Says It Bees That Way Sometimes "Pet Peeves: The Sequel" by Downtown Bruno.**

This one is for the boys or "so called" boys who want to call themselves wrestlers, even though they never made their living in MY profession/business/industry/sport. There are two sets of guys in the indy circuit.

#1: Guys who have the desire, drive, potential to actually make a living in our industry – Kid Nikels, Eric Wayne, Matt Boyce, Kevin White, Moe Stegall, Derrick King, Austin Lane etc – you get the idea??

#2: There are guys who don't know their ass from their elbow who think they are actually IN the business because they work some little bulls**t show for some bulls**t promotion. They are the big turd in a small toilet. Guess f**king what?? You are no more a wrestler by doing that than I am a f**king pilot just because I fly a lot.

Another thing – if you think you are a f**king wrestler – buy some damn tights, pads, etc!! In our f**king day, if you didn't have proper gear – you didn't have a JOB!! Also, if you are a hobbyist, leave me alone!! No, I can't get you booked in the WWE. I can't get you a tryout. I can't get you to meet Vince/Johnny/Stephanie/etc. Get it yourself – I did!! Earn it!! If you never did anything full time or even semi time, then how the hell do you think you are ready for the major league?? Pick up hoops = NBA?? Little League = MLB?? You would get ate up like a hamburger in New York – trust me!!

I can hear it now. Who the f**k do I think I am?? I am washed up!! I don't know what I am talking about! Fine! Have fun in front of 90 people! I have been on top or 2nd to the top at four Wrestlemanias!! And I still make a good living in WWE! You?? I didn't think so. Learn your craft, stop knocking NEW and realize that it's the only f**king place around here to actually LEARN how to make a living in the business. You might…MIGHT....have a shot! Take it from a has-been – you can't be a has-been if you are a never-was. Think about that – it might come to you!

**-Jerry Lawler files lawsuit versus Corey Maclin over video footage. From 7.12.10 editon of Wrestling Global Newsletter by Mike Aldren.**

Jerry Lawler is suing former business associate and promoter Cory Maclin over the rights to the Memphis Wrestling video tape library. The story dates back two years when Maclin licensed footage to a tape trader to produce a 20 volume DVD set titled "Corey Maclin presents Memphis Wrestling". Lawler, who found out about the DVD deal last August, says that Maclin has no rights to license any footage because he, Lawler, purchased them along with the USWA promotion from

Jerry Jarrett in 1996. Who exactly owns the Memphis library has been a contentious issue for years. Very few broadcast-quality betacam tapes still exist, but the rights would be owned by either Lawler, Jarrett, or possibly a Cleveland-based company, XL Sports, that purchased the USWA from Lawler and a guy called Larry Burton in 1997, that later went out of business, resulting in a nasty lawsuit between all three. "To have someone you actually put into the wrestling business come back and do something like Corey has done is really disappointing," said Lawler. "I'm not worried about ownership of the footage because you can't own stolen property, which in essence is what this boils down to." Maclin released a statement which said he believes the suit is politically motivated because he's currently running for office in Tennessee. He is challenging Lawler to prove ownership. He also said his personal issues with him started in 2007, when a Lawler vs. Hulk Hogan event fell apart when Lawler pulled out citing his contractual obligations to WWE. Maclin later sued WWE, claiming the company put pressure on Lawler to withdraw from the event. Lawler's suit follows a recent cease and desist letter from Maclin demanding that his image never appear on Lawler's new Memphis Wrestling television show. Maclin says he wants to distance himself from people in the wrestling business. Said Maclin, "I believe that this lawsuit is political in nature. I always knew that Jerry was a Republican, but was stunned to find out that he had a sign in his yard supporting a man that as far as I know has never met my opponent in the race for Clerk of Shelby County. I can no longer promote or support Jerry Lawler personally or professionally. I am saddened by the people he has chosen to associate with and can no longer be a part of any project Mr. Lawler is involved with."

**-RRO Memphis Wrestling Hall of Famer Bobby Eaton is hospitalized.**

**-EWE returns to Ripley, TN with no Derrick King and booked by Jon Michael.**

**-Tony Dabbs beats Neil Taylor to win TFW Title when Gene Jackson interferes and turns on Taylor. 7.09.10**

**-Jon Michael has a seizure that sidelines him for a few months.**

----I talked with Jon Michael a bit tonight. He had a big scare today with a seizure. He is to see a specialist and will be able to give us an update. He has been told not to drive, swim, or wrestle. He told me he was conscious during the whole ordeal. Our thoughts are with Jon Michael and hope for a speedy recovery. He wrote the following on Facebook today...

*please keep me in your prayers. earlier today, i had a very rare and bad seizure. my body went into shock, i began bleeding from the nose or mouth. i'm hurting and i honestly thought i was going to die. I was concious for the whole thing yelling uncontrolabley. Please say a smal prayer for me, i'm scared.*

**-Sir Mo films Xplosive Championship Wrestling debut in Newbern, TN 7.18.10**

**-Prime-Time Wrestling show in Memphis, TN draws close to 100 with Alan Steele vs Flash Flanagan main event. 7.16.10**

-Sid Vicious wrestled Loose Cannon for MCW.

-"The Golden Boy" Greg Anthony wins EWE beating Christian Jacobs in EWE return.  Ripley, TN 7.16.10

-The Golden Circle "Masturbation Match" by Greg Anthony.

*I want feedback from you guys on this one*

I can only imagine the pissed off people around the world that will type "masturbation" into google and come up with a link to this article, because it isn't as dirty as it sounds.  A masturbation match is something we've all done.  It's that match we do just for us.  We don't care what the crowd wants, needs or even knows.  And just like the literal meaning, it may fulfill some short term desire, but whether in life or wrestling, masturbating doesn't make the world work.

I've been a part of many matches where I was more trying to keep up with the Jones' than really tuned in to my audience.  I wanted to prove to myself, not really anyone in particular, that I was as good or even better than some guy up East that's featured somewhere.  When I started to really listen to the people, that's when I became able to predict their reactions more.  That's when my work started to grow.

Psychologists study for years.  They learn people's actions and reactions to every possible situation so they can help and treat.  But they learn all of this from a book.  We as wrestlers are a poor man's psychologist.  We go out and instead of reading about a reaction, we provoke it.  As a wrestling fan I've laughed, cried, been angry, betrayed, seen and felt the pain of infidelity, nepotism and probably everything that's in that magical textbook.

I've seen so many guys go out there and do a bunch of nonsensical gibberish that didn't help anything.  Didn't help them or their opponent get over, didn't entertain the crowd, and at the end of the day isn't going to sell one more ticket.  It was an expression of self love.  So good job on the masturbation match.  Now wipe yourself off, and try to do something productive next time.

Once again, just like masturbation we all do it.  Maybe not so much a whole match anymore, but maybe a masturbation spot.  Just to squeeze one out and get on to the job at hand.  So don't feel too guilty, just think what would happen to the world if all we did was masturbate?  The human race would die off, and so would wrestling.  I promise.

-Cody Murdoch suffers injury that sidelines him for rest of the year.

-Bobby Eaton inducted into ASWF Hall of Fame 7.24.10

**-Arena Report NEW West Memphis , AR 7.23.10**

----Dan Matthews beat Jon Allen...Justin Smart beat Kevin Charles...Eric Wayne beat Moe Stegall by KO...Austin Lane/Kid Nikels beat Chris Stryker/Shawn Reed.

For Full Report and notes go to: *Yearbook 2010 Web Companion*

**-"Asylum" [Psycho/Pappy] win NWA Southern Tag Team Titles and Tasha Simone wins NWA Ladies Title Lebanon, TN 7.24.10**

**-Bad Brad Simpson beats Way Cool to win TIWF Title. 7.24.10**

**-TV Ratings for RCW and ASWF released.**

----I got some info about the ratings for both the RCW and ASWF TV shows that air on Channel 8 in Jonesboro, AR. I really did not expect much with the show airing at 12:30am on a Saturday night, and honestly they are not great. The DMA avg. is a 1 rating with an 8 share, and a 13 HUT. What that means is that about 8% of the people watching TV at that time of night were watching (RCW). In other words, out of the 10,800 people in the entire area watching TV at that time, about 865 were watching RCW. I was told that's the best you can expect for such a bad time slot.

----ASWF got roughly the same number on Friday night, but there were fewer people watching TV that night. They got a 1 rating, with an 11 share, but only a 5 HUT. It works out to about 4,150 people watching TV at that timeslot, so they've got about 455 viewers.

----At this point both promotions will have to decide if TV is helping their product with less than 1000 people watching it. At this point, RCW is on a hiatus from running house shows right now and have enough in their can to continue to run TV shows. Not sure about ASWF, but SOMETHING has been helping them draw fans to the shows. I think it can be contributed to TV [hardcore fans], no wrestling in Jonesboro, and new talent in ASWF like Brian Christopher.

**-Coach's Corner "Psychology 102" by Brian Tramel**

----So, in the summer of 2007, I ventured to Mississippi to sit through a marathon of matches. When I got back, I was totally disgusted. It really happens every time I go to watch wrestling in Mississippi. I posted an article titled, "Psychology 101: The Simple Plan" in *Yearbook 2007*, [page 67] and it was well received by most on the site. It was just a basic structure to what a match is SUPPOSED to be. In the years that have followed, I have noticed that the basic structure of matches has improved in this area. If this site has contributed anything to this area, it is the constant preaching of improving the quality by not only me, but my whole staff. There is something I have noticed though. The workers do have the basics down, but after that there seems to be no creativity. The art of going from basic psychology in a match to having great matches is a process that only the worker can improve. So, I have some ways to improve your matches – listen to the crowd, watch matches, and ask questions.

----At "Summer Breakout" in Newbern, TN in June, the opening bout is the perfect example of listening to the crowd. Blaine Devine worked Oz. They had a real good opening bout. The crowd was into the match with the fans really into Oz. The guys did a typical match with basic psychology. Their psychology was perfect. You got to remember guys – you know the outcome of the match, but the crowd does not – so build for that. In this situation, the crowd was sooo hot for Oz that I suggested they go longer with the babyface shine. Let Oz get more and more. Devine was going over in the end, so why not let Oz get as much as he wanted? In the end, it makes Devine look even better, because he is going over Oz. [Oz got all those moves over on Devine, but Devine beat him anyway] The crowd will tell you when it is time to move on. It works in tag team matches also. If the crowd is not there for the hot tag, then they will stay flat. If you go out there and go too long or you give them too many false hot tags, then they wear out. You have to know that when it is time to happen, it should be hot all around and the crowd should be up. If you do not accomplish that, then the hot tag means nothing.

----The modern invention of www.youtube.com has made it easy to learn from others. Type names like Arn Anderson, Bret Hart, Ricky Steamboat, Armstrong [Scott/Brad] and Ricky Morton into the search engine. These were normal size guys that knew how to sell and work. Anderson was primarily a heel in his career, and he is an example of a smaller guy that can get over as a heel. Tag teams like Midnight Express, Rock N Roll Express, The Nightmares, Demolition [big guys that could work] and Heavenly Bodies are great examples. Study the way the guys come in and out of heat. Study how they get the hot tag. Study how they pace the bout. Study the moves and holds. Study…Study…Study!! When you watch RAW or TNA, do the same thing – watch the basics and how many different ways they do things. I am so sick of seeing people imitating Randy Orton's arms wide open taunt. Or how about coming out of heat without hitting an enzuigiri?? Can you do ONE match without a superkick?? You know a heel can be smarter than a babyface?? Babyface can just screw up a move for the heel to take over; right? If you watch ROH stuff or any other promotion that might do these super out of the world moves, then steal one of them as your finisher. You don't want to just throw it in so it makes you look good. It will look a lot better if you get a move from a promotion that is not watched by the majority of your fans, instead of stealing a signature move from a WWE guy.

----Many guys don't like asking the old pros for advice, because at times guys will just say everything sucks. I would be more than happy to give you a one on one critique of your match. If Flash Flanagan, Derrick King, Greg Anthony, Pokerface, Rude, Alan Steele, Kevin White or someone that has experience and is recognized as a good worker is in your dressing room – ask them to watch your match. They will be fair and tell you what they would have done. They can tell you what you are doing wrong. And if they say you suck, then you pretty much suck. LOL! When these guys take their time to watch your match and you want the input, listen and shut up. I hate it when I am asked to watch a match, I tell them what they did wrong, and that person says, "Yeah…I know…" If you KNOW, then why the hell do you keep doing it?? Another good way of asking questions is just to watch the matches from top to bottom on your show if you are able to do so. This will give you the chance to see what others are doing, so you don't do the same finish or come out of heat the same way. And you may ask questions to the guys like "why did you do that?" It also gives you the chance to pick up extra tips about working a match.

----You can go from the basics of just doing Psychology 101 to being a better worker. If you got the basics down and you understand the whys and the hows, then it is time to learn other ways of perfecting your craft. Listening to the crowd, watching other matches and asking questions will help you go from the basics to the old pro.

**-XCW show canceled at ASWF's Valiant Arena when Sir Mo and ASWF owner David Walls have a disagreement.**

## JULY PHOTOS

**Top row from left: Jon Michael, Justin Smart and "LSD"**

**Bottom from left: Greg Anthony, Jeremy Moore and Devon Day/Kilo**

## AUGUST

-Alan Steele appears in *A Day in the Life of a Professional Wrestler* DVD.

-Friday Night Wrestling promotion announced to debut October 1st in Memphis, TN.

-TIWF wrestler Billy Joe Bishop dies after 2 ½ year battle with cancer. Bishop wrestled as Billy Joe Dream and Razor. 8.04.10

-Corey Maclin loses local election.

-Big night at MCW when Pokerface beats Rik Burton to win MCW Title and then loses title to Lord Humongous. Frankie Tucker/Big Daddy LaFonce beat V-Man/Officer Hudson. 8.06.10

-Arena Report: Benefit @ NEW Arena West Memphis, AR 8.14.10

----Dustin Ring beat Seth Knight…Justin Smart/Dustin Ring beat "Prime Danger" [Dan Matthews/Kevin Charles]…Alan Steele beat Tatt2…Greg Anthony beat Moe Stegall… Eric Wayne vs Kid Nikels went to a time limit draw… Austin Lane beat "TGB" Greg Anthony

Full Report and notes go to: *Yearbook 2010 Web Companion*

-RCW no longer on TV.

-Eric Wayne films part for a movie at Crystal Palace skating rink.

-Coach's Corner XXL "Passion and Common Sense" by Brian Tramel.

----It's been a hectic couple of weeks here at the RRO offices with the site being on fire with hits, because of various reasons. I have read and listened to a ton of people on all the controversial topics. I have had texts, calls, and e-mails in almost record numbers. What I consider a hobby is sometimes more of a part-time job when weeks like this happen at the site. After taking a week to absorb everything that I read - Sir Mo to David Walls to EPW to Jeremy Wood to Jeremy Moore to Eric Wayne, I remembered the passion that this sport births. It is like a disease in the blood. Or it has even been compared to the mafia before – you can say "I quit," but you can NEVER leave. Passion can sometimes equal a huge success and at other times can equal you climbing out of a window when someone's husband comes home. That passion, though, just reminded me of the steps that some of us have gone through just to be part of this business.

----First let me tell you about this kid I once knew. He was around 19 years old and he wrote for the old kayfabe sheets. He always loved wrestling and his new found awareness of what was going on backstage, just made him want to learn more. He was a major source for the top wrestling kayfabe sheet in the business – Wrestling Observer Newsletter. He was Dave Meltzer's Memphis source. He also contributed to Yearbooks and was very critical of Memphis Wrestling. Well, one night after Jerry Lawler had read some stuff he wrote, he called him into the dressing room to threaten to kick his ass and tell him that he was a piece of s**t. He told him that he would never wrestle and never be anyone. That kid dropped about 30 lbs, trained in the gym and then trained with another guy to wrestle at least one match. In his mind, if he could wrestle just one match, then he would prove to Lawler that he could wrestle. He wrestled that one match, and then went on to work for about 18 months as a wrestler. An untrained, unskilled, fat, horrible wrestler. After taking a weekend to look over his matches, he made a decision – he sucked in the ring and was just an embarrassment to the wrestling business. Lawler was right – he would never be a wrestler. His passion got him this far, but his common sense told him he should not be a wrestler.

----Let me tell you also about a guy that in his mid 30's decided he wanted to be part of the wrestling business. His friend was a professional wrestler and was training a few guys. After the training was over, he decided to help the guys and then decided to manage them. He got to live his dream by just watching them in the ring. They could do things he could NEVER do. He could not train a guy on holds or moves. He could not tell them exactly what to do in the matches, but he could help them. He watched as many matches as he could get his hands on, and he would help them with psychology. He would book them shows. He would help write their storylines. He traveled up and down the roads with them for almost five years. He bumped in almost every match. He would come out with every one of them and make a bunch of noise. He would try to be the center of attention. After a long look at his matches and such, he finally realized that even though everyone was tooting his horn, he was not a great manager. He won awards voted on by the fans – Manager of the Year for two years. But, after listening to a few people, he decided his brand of managing was not as effective as it could be. His passion got him this far, but his common sense told him that he was never going to do anything big in the business and his body was taking too much punishment. He decided to hang it up.

----This other guy I know, he was also in his 30's when he decided he wanted to be a wrestling promoter. He took a crew of guys – most of them very green - and ran local towns with them. He wrote his own storylines, and booked the shows around the talent that would work for him. He enjoyed his shows and he saw some success, but nothing major. He ran shows for almost two years and even to this day the guys that worked for him are still his friends. The guys have nothing but fond memories of their time spent with this promoter. Ok, maybe he was an asshole sometimes, but most of them will admit – they learned something and would work for this guy again. Did he pay well? Nah. Did he do everything perfect?? Nah. Did he keep himself out of the ring and let actual wrestlers work?? Nah. Well...ok...most of the time – he honestly worked only a few matches and at times managed some of the heels. Did he put his wife in the ring and push her when he shouldn't have?? Yeah. Did he want to do everything his way? Yeah. Was he good at what he did?? Not really or he would probably still be promoting. He ended up going through a nasty divorce and selling the ring. His passion got him that far, but his common sense told him that he was not a great promoter, so he better stay out of it.

----Finally, let me tell you about this last guy. He had toyed with the idea of starting a website for a few years. He was a former wrestling kayfabe sheet guy, wrestler, manager and promoter. He was not highly successful in any of those things, but he honestly loved the wrestling business in this area. This guy was closing in on turning 40 years old and it was time for him to either say goodbye to his childhood fantasy of wrestling or do something to help this area. He is not always right. He has at times done stories that he is not proud of. He has had to cover deaths of guys that he has been fans of his whole life. And deaths of friends. He has had to write about fights in dressing rooms. Fights in the crowd by wrestlers or wrestlers' wives. He has been threatened. He has been told everything about his site from "you do a great job" to "you are piece of s\*\*t." In one night he can have a legend say he does a great job and then turn around to hear another one tell him he doesn't know what he is talking about. He has made friends, but none of them are ABOVE the site and he has lost a few because of that. Above everything he tries to make the guys in this area seem to be a big deal. He wants them to mean something. He wants them to succeed, because even though he might be accused of being bad for wrestling, he loves this business. He has published books because of the site – something he always wanted to do. His common sense sometimes tells him to stop spending so much time and effort on the site, but his passion keeps him doing it.

----For those still with me for this XXL edition of *Coach's Corner*, you have probably already figured out that all those stories are about one person – me. My passion for this business has not made me a rich man, but it has given me memories that will stay with me for life. Many people grow up wanting to be something. They want to be a rock star, a fireman, a policeman…or like me and many people reading this – I wanted to be in the wrestling business. And, I can honestly say I have spent the better part of my adult life feeling like a part of this brotherhood. For people like me that have a passion for this business, it is hard to hear the word "No" or be told "you can not do that" because you want it so bad. If you are a promoter or money mark, then promote and do what you can. But, please stay out of the ring. If you are not a trained wrestler, then don't put anyone in the ring and try to train them – send them somewhere to get properly trained. If you can honestly watch your matches and say they are as good as what you have seen on TV, then stick with it. Please use your brain and if you suck – do us all a favor and throw those tights away that don't fit you anyway. And, please, put on a damn shirt so we don't have to look at your skinny ass body!! There is a place for everyone in this business with desire. You can help set up the ring, sell popcorn, take pictures, ring announce, rent a building, work the front door or even start your own website. Let a lesson be learned here though – don't let your passion make you lose your common sense.

**-Wrestling Trainee Jeremy Wood dies after training session. 8.15.10**

**-Jeremy Wood – Timeline and My Thoughts**

----On **Thursday, 8.12.10** it was reported that SWA trainee Jeremy Wood was injured during a training session in Newport, AR where his trainer was being "rough" on him. He had fallen on his neck and was rushed to the hospital.

----Later that day, I posted that Wood had a fractured skull and is being sedated for the next three days. Apparently everyone believed he would be ok when they woke him up from the sedation.

----The promotion issued a statement later that day.

Dear Mr.Tramel:

Mr.Wood was not roughed up and he did not fall on his neck. He got over heated, got out of the ring to set down and had a seizure, he's still in the hospital with blood on his brain but will be ok and hopefully released in a few days. I have been getting negative calls and text messages all day about people reading this and believing we beat his a**. Mr. Tramel if you could please correct this because I don't want people reading false information about this guy or my company.

**Friday 8.13.10**

----I just got off the phone with ASWF owner David Walls and he just spoke with the father of Jeremy Wood. Here is what Walls was told:

-Jeremy has blue and red marks of hand prints of at least 5 different hands from chops.

-He has not been conscious since the training session.

-He was powerbombed by Cujo.

-He hit the mat so hard that it separated his lungs.

-He has bleeding on his brain.

----We will keep following this story as closely as we can. Our thoughts are with the family and Jeremy.

----I also talked with Cujo who said this incident occurred after a series of front rolls. He got out of the ring and what is believed was a seizure happened next. Cujo commented that people offered him water or Gatorade. All he did was front rolls and closelines. The chop marks were actually from the day before.

----On **Sunday, August 15, 2010,** I posted the following...

----Here is something that I got from a reliable source. Jeremy's grandma was at the SWA show Friday night. SWA gave all the door money to their family to help with hospital bills. She thanked Cujo and Sam Lassiter for their help. They were told he DID NOT have a skull fracture, but had a concussion and a seizure. The local hospital has him sedated because they thought he might have a fractured skull. That source also stated, "NO ONE was trying to be a "tough guy" and beat up the kid.

----Terrance Ward then published the following along with the photo below on Tuesday, 8.17.10.

I along with David Walls of the ASWF, and close family friend of Jeremy Wood's family, spoke with Jeremy's father Sunday afternoon. I was told his condition is still the same and is paralyzed on one side of his body and one of his eyes is paralyzed. We were also told by his father that he is apparently aware that he is in the hospital after trying to remove the ventilator that is helping him breath. David, Jeremy's dad, also stated that you can wake him now but he can't talk.

This picture [go to *Yearbook 2010 Web Companion* to find link] was sent to me by e-mail and I think that it needs to be shared to show the severity of his injuries and prove to speculators that Jeremy is NOT okay. We here in the Mid-South and those that keep up with Wrestling News Center wish Jeremy a speedy recovery and hopes that God helps you through your tough recovery.

**Wednesday, 8.18.10**

----Then it is reported, less than a week after the incident that the family removed the breathing machine and Jeremy Wood was pronounced dead.

**MY THOUGHTS**

----Ok, what the hell happened?? How does a guy go from being trained to dead within a week?? Something went wrong. And guess what?? We are never going to know. I got tons of people that I talked to within the last few days that want to go after Cujo. But, what if it happened the way they are saying it happened?? If they did NOTHING to hurt him?? How did he end up paralyzed and dead?? Could this have been from an existing medical condition?? If everyone had thought he was too small or too sick to train, then why train him? On the other hand, we have been told he was part of the National Guard. If so, then they would not have a guy who was unhealthy – physically or mentally – would they??

----I have even had people ask me, "What really happened?" And, I honestly have posted everything I know about the situation. Everyone is going to have their own opinion and it will be hard to be able to tell what the **REAL** story is, especially if you have an official investigation, criminal charges and such.

----A few things I want to stress though. Please understand the importance of training with an official training facility. I do think there are a few individuals that can personally train people in this area, but if you go to a facility such as Kevin White's school or the Ken Wayne Nightmare School of Wrestling, then you will be treated professionally. I am not saying accidents do not happen and if this kid had an existing medical condition, then you might say it could have happened at those schools also. But, no, because White/Wayne are not going to train you if you are not physically able to do it.

----I never met Jeremy. All the people that knew him only had good things to say about him. They said he LOVED wrestling and just wanted to be part of it. It really saddened me to report his death, because I was hoping he would be ok. My thoughts are with his family and friends. If his death was because of the negligence of others, I do hope you are punished. If the family decides this was not the fault of the training, then I really hope the wrestling community gets behind them and tries to help everyone get over it.

**MORE coverage**

----I would like to say that as of last Saturday, the sources on the side of the "training camp" have pretty much dried up. I am not sure if they have been told not to talk, but I have not heard anything from anyone. I was supposed to get more comments from Cujo on various things, but he never did send anything. I also contacted a few people that claimed to be there during the training session and all of them declined to talk.

**-Mama Says It Bees That Way Sometimes "Legit Training" by Downtown Bruno**

You know what? After what happened to Jeremy Wood in Arkansas last week, we should all feel silly...myself included...for actually taking up time,or should I say WASTING time, concerning ourselves with stupid bulls**t that really doesn't matter at all in the big scheme of things. All of us who read this site and participate in professional wrestling have some stake in this profession, whether it's making a living at it, wanting to make a living at it, or hopefully just trying to contribute to the business. Also, hopefully, trying to learn and improve every time they get around the business and people that they can learn from. If you don't fit into any of these categories, then you don't belong in the ring - period! And that's something I don't think anybody would expect me to apologize for!

Jeremy Wood was a young man who I only met once, briefly, when I first participated in an ASWF event in Tuckerman, AR. I don't claim to be a good friend of his or even to know him, but in the brief, vague time we met, I do know that he was respectful to me and my wife. This goes without saying, he obviously loved the business and wanted to be a part of it in some way, and in the end, that's what killed him. Because he was obviously in the ring with people who didn't have the proper knowledge, skill, or perhaps, wherewithal to train him properly, and now he's dead!!!

I never thought I'd have to write that sentence about ANYBODY! Ok, if he was only in his 2nd session of training, why in the world was he doing clotheslines and taking powerbombs, as has been reported? Obviously, I wasn't there, so I can only comment on the rumors and gossip that's going around, but if that's the case, that's the most irresponsible and unprofessional thing I have ever heard in 31 years of making my LIVING at this! Powerbombs are advanced moves...clotheslines come later in training, too. You start out by forward rolls, hitting the ropes, learning to lock up, etc. If you are going for your driving test, you don't learn Nascar manuevers or demolition derby tactics, do you? Hell no!!!!!!!

Please, everybody, if you want to be in this business. PLEASE go to a reputable training facility that is run by somebody that has actually been in the business, not some jerk-off in jeans and a t-shirt who knows about as much as the people sitting in the audience. Of course, Nightmare Ken Wayne has a great school that I highly recommend to one and all, but there is also Kevin White and Brian Christopher who are great guys and great hands in the ring who can send you in the right direction as well. Lance Storm, Harley Race, Steve Keirn, Sir Mo, Rodney Mack, Rick Bassman and a host of others. They actually get it, and do it right. Stay away from the ones that have never walked the walk, because, sadly as we have all found out this week - they will not just take your money and train you wrong, which is bad enough in and of itself, but.....sadly...they can kill you. GOD rest poor J. Wood, and pray for his family. Thank you.

An additional comment I would like to put on this great site is just that now that all the Downtown Bruno/EPW controversy has been addressed, dealt with, apologized about and moved on, I will not be posting ANY more comments on Hollywood Jimmy's message board. Anything I have to say will be either on RRO or WNC, so it can be verified by Jimmy and Brian Tramel that it indeed is me. That it is not somebody trying to start a bunch of crap! Therefore, if anybody posts anything on the message board or anyplace else besides rro or wnc, I can promise you that it's not me, it's an impostor. Why the hell would somebody want to pretend to be me? Pretend to be Brad Pitt or George Clooney for Christ's sake, you'll get more results,at least till you are exposed!!!! LOL!!!

**-Coach's Corner "Call To Arms" by Brian Tramel**

----This site can be accused of many things. I am accused of "starting s**t" or at least stirring it. I have been told that I don't know anything about the wrestling business, but in the same breath I have been told I "get it." It is hard to have real friends when you are considered the "press", and some guys will just quit talking to me when I do not write good things about them. I will then be bashed until I actually say something good about them again, and then "bam" I am their friend again. My objectivity is questioned at times, but I think this site is able to give you news, gossip, opinion and results all wrapped up into a TMZ meets Wall Street Journal package. The current story with Jeremy Wood has been a true test of my objectivity and patience in sitting back and letting the story unfold without making judgment either way. Since I cannot tell you what happened the day Jeremy died or the day before he died, I cannot honestly give a judgment. The one thing I can do though, is to ask that we as a wrestling community band together to make sure that this sort of thing does not happen again.

**----Two cases we have to look at:**

-January 2007,: Nick Halpin, 28, was reportedly practicing moves with several other individuals when he fell unconscious. A 911 call Sunday from the New Blood Wrestling arena noted Halpin was suffering from heat exhaustion. Halpin died the next day. No negligence was found in this case.

-August, 2010: Jeremy Wood, 20, was reportedly practicing moves with several other individuals when he fell unconscious.  Wood would be pronounced dead the Wednesday after the incident.  Lt. Weatherford with the Newport Police Department stated in the KARK piece,

*"Right now, after interviewing these people, we are not able to point our finger at any specific person or event that caused Mr. Wood's injuries."*

----So, if both of these deaths are considered to have no negligence, is there still something that the wrestling community can do??  As I said, we need to band together with everyone involved - TV shows, promoters, commission, workers and RRO to find ways to ensure these tragedies are not repeated.

-TV Shows:  The area currently airs TV with NEW and Jerry Lawler's Memphis Wrestling.  Both of these shows need to step up and take some time to record a PSA [Public Service Announcement] to air on their TV shows.  All it has to be is a 30 second spot featuring either the promoter or the workers saying things like, "Do not do these moves unless you are trained" and "if you want to become a professional wrestler, then please be trained by a professional."  I think this would be very effective coming from guys like Jerry Lawler and Ken Wayne.  If guys on Memphis Wrestling like Kevin White and Brian Christopher, who run a school, could come totally out of character, it would make the message seem stronger.

-Promoters:  Please have your announcers make weekly announcements to tell the fans the same as in a PSA.  Promoters also have to get an approved list of wrestling trainers that the whole community will support.  The problem is that if you as promoter make the announcement, but then you have "Joe-Bob" become your head trainer, then you are just part of the problem.  When someone asks to be trained, you should be able to hand them a piece of paper with contact numbers, instead of telling him to show up before the show next week and we will beat you up type of thing.  Also, as a promoter, you need to make sure your crew are professionally trained.  Your crew should be representatives of these approved schools.  Don't put people in the ring that do not belong in the ring, just because you are trying to cut the budget.  Do you think Ken Wayne or Jerry Lawler put guys in the ring that are not trained??

-Commission:  There is a fine line here between TOO much and NOTHING.  I believe there should exist a commission, but most commissions are one of two things.  #1: They are so strict and treat wrestling as a total shoot that small promotions can not survive such as the commission in Missouri.  #2: They exist just to get money and have no other real purpose.  And in some states, a commission doesn't even exist.  I think a person participating weekly in wrestling shows should be able to at least pass a physical exam.   You must pass that to participate in high school sports, but not professional wrestling??  Promoters also have to step up here and get licensed as a promotion with all licensed workers.  So, we need a commission to at least ask something of the promotions such as a physical, instead of just taking everyone's money.

-Workers:  As a wrestler in this area, you have to step up and take some responsibility.  Everyone is not going to be able to train guys.  You can't just take someone's money and promise them you are going to make them a wrestler.  And if the promoters would actually step up to this, then your normal "Joe-Bob" is not going to get you anywhere. As soon as a worker does not say he has been trained by the approved list, then as a promoter, as a fellow worker - YOU do not get to wrestle!! If you do train someone, you have to be a professional, instead of just doing super moves or beating the hell out of a new guy. You have to be approved by the community.

-RRO: I am willing to become the center of all of this change that needs to happen. The promoters, training centers and such have a central location that they can share information. There needs to be a meeting of sorts [even if it has to be via e-mail] that all the promoters sit down and make a decision on who trains and who is considered approved. This site is viewed by all the promoters in this area and 95% of the workers. If I can help to arrange some kind of seminar, meeting or PSA to help this problem, then I will be there to help. I plan to do my part at all the live events that attend in upcoming months and also during the Yearbook Tour in 2011.

-----Can there be a change?? Will the promoters, commission and workers in this area jump in to solve this problem? I know in the past promotions in this area do not seem to be able to work together, but this is a time that everyone needs to put aside their differences and make a difference. Do we really need more people dying to get something done??

**-Corey Maclin reports to new job as WPTY/WLMT Sports director.**

**-Derrick King leaves Memphis Wrestling.**

----Whether you want to say "fired" or "quit" or whatever, Derrick King is no longer working for Memphis Wrestling. King, who has been a prominent fixture on Memphis Wrestling TV, has not been used for the last two JLMW TV tapings.

----The problems all started when rumors of a show being run in Memphis, TN at the New Daisy surfaced. "Friday Night Wrestling" debuts on October 1, 2010 advertising  TNA Star/Sharkboy, Former WWE/WCW/TNA Champion/ Kid Kash, Former WWE/TNA Legend/ Road Dogg Jesse James, Former WWE/TNA Star "The Natural" Chase Stevens, Memphis Legend/Dangerous Doug Gilbert and some local guys like Tatt2, Derrick King, Cody Melton, Precious and more.

----As the show was being announced Jerry Lawler was told that Wolfie D, Derrick King and Cody Melton were planning to work the show. Lawler allegedly, as I was told, "crawled Wolfie's ass" about being on the show. Lawler putting it to Wolfie and anyone else - if you work the New Daisy show, then you don't work for Memphis Wrestling.

----Lawler was apparently even offered a spot on the New Daisy show to judge a "Divas" contest, but turned it down. The promotion also wanted Brian Christopher to work the show. Lawler sees this as someone coming into your town to do a show [competition], since he has plans to run house shows in the future. Lawler was very adamant during the initial WWE expansion and when WCW would run shows in Memphis. None of the wrestlers were permitted to go to the shows and he even forbade his own children from attending the shows.

----"I am not knocking them. I just want to do some different." Derrick King told RRO. So, King has elected to work "Friday Night Wrestling" over JLMW. It is not clear which group would benefit King at this point in his career, but he is doing something quite "different" this time. King has been a mainstay of Memphis Wrestling for years and been well known as a "good hand", a team player, and considered a Lawler supporter.

----King will only be missing actually one payoff a month with JLMW tapings and is wrestling close to a full schedule right now. He is working four nights this coming week. Cody Melton looks to be working the New Daisy show, and Wolfie D is sticking with Memphis Wrestling.

**-Jeremy Wood is buried. 8.30.10**

## AUGUST PHOTOS

Top row left: Bobby Eaton, Jerry Lawler and Gary Valiant

Bottom row left: Blaine Devine [Rick Nelson: Printmaster Photography], Tat2 [Rick Nelson: Printmaster Photography] and Tasha Simone

## SEPTEMBER

**-WREG Channel 3 airs a piece on Jeremy Wood.**

**-Sign posted at Delta Fair causes controversy.**

----A picture {September photos page] was sent in from the Delta Fair. IWA had their ring set up a couple hundred yards from the building where JLMW was set up. When this picture was taken - two little kids, maybe 8 or 9, were getting in the ring and throwing each other around. At one point one kid used a headlock takedown that nearly drove the little kid's head in the mat and what resembled a firemans carry/DVD or whatever. Very "cute" and dangerous and STUPID!!

**-Jerry Lawler's Memphis Wrestling is dead.**

----As reported earlier on www.wrestlingnewscenter.com today, Jerry Lawler's Memphis Wrestling will not air after this weekend's show.

----Rich reported the following...

*I talked to Hollywood Jimmy after the show last night to confirm the story and he told me it's true. He wouldn't go into details the reason the show is going off the air but said there are a few problems and if a miracle doesn't take place within a few days the show airing this Saturday will be the last Jerry Lawler's Memphis Wrestling show.*

----This is a story that I have been working on since about the middle of last week. I knew that Jerry Lawler would be informing talent on Sunday night on the future of the promotion, and felt it was not something to report until talent was told it was ending.

----As Rich said, if something does not drastically change in the next few days, this coming Saturday is the last day. The reason for this is simple. Money going out was going to be more than money coming in. Jerry Lawler is not going to lose money to keep a weekly show on in Memphis when it is only being seen by 11,000 people.

----Apparently, Joe Cooper [Lawler's partner], arranged for 12 weeks of advertising. Lawler and Cooper had a "break up" of sorts over a new wrestling themed deli that was supposed to open with Lawler's name in mid August. This led to Cooper not negotiating to get new sponsors or renewing the current ones. The last two shows would be Lawler finishing up what sponsorship obligations he has and putting his own money into those shows.

-Memphis Wrestling draws 632 for show at Delta Fair with Jerry Lawler vs Reggie B Fine main event. 9.05.10  Go to *Yearbook 2010 Web Companion.*

-The Straight Flush "I Really Hope I Offend Someone…" by Pokerface

For the last couple of weeks, the Jeremy Wood incident has been on everyone's lips, even the media. I've heard and read all the rumors. Now it's time for me to give my thoughts. I really hope that I do offend somebody.

Last week on this site, I watched the news report on Jeremy. By nature, I'm an emotional guy. This story actually brought tears to my eyes. It couldn't have come at a worse time. I was getting ready to leave for a show that evening. Anyway, seeing pictures of that young man laying in that bed on life support really tugged at my heart. Then I went from being sad to extremely angry, because years ago, I was Jeremy Woods. I was a wild-eyed kid who would've done anything or let anyone train me, as long as I could get in the business. It's a shame that you got stupid motherf**kers who have no ring presence, no charisma, no drawing power or potential, and no talent training people. And the one who allegedly is the main one at fault, isn't even qualified to run the concession stand, let alone wrestle. I know this because I used to wrestle in the same company as this guy. Wrestlers think that the fact that they can hip toss somebody makes them a qualified trainer. And now since they didn't have a clue or know-how, a father and mother are without their son. This pisses me off as a father and a wrestler.

I consider myself a helluva wrestler, and in my opinion, one of the best. But I would not train anybody. There are alot of great workers in this area. But remember, good players don't always make good coaches. I have no patience and have a hard time explaining things. I can do cool s**t in the ring, but if you ask me how, 9 times out of 10 I couldn't tell you. Anyway, I've been asked by a lot of people to train them, and I politely decline. I always refer them to one of two places in this area, because I know my limitations. The closest I've come to training someone was a female trainee in Jonesboro. She was a student of Rodney Mack. He would train her during the week, and on Saturdays before the show I would work with her, not as a trainer, but a tutor. I would just reinforce what she was already taught. Plus I would just go over the basics, i.e chain wrestling, and drills. When we do mass training or working out, I would be in charge of the physical training, and I would be instructed on what drill or areas to take the guys through. And it was all a team effort. All vets and not-so-vets contributed to the session, under one teacher.

Over the years I've seen guys who weren't even a year into the business training people. What the f**k! I've seen guys who have been wrestling for 10+ years, who still can't work, training people. What the f**k! Get real. Anyway, when I was watching the news story, it pretty much said that nobody that was at the training session when Jeremy allegedly got powerbombed 25 times is talking. Pussies! I'm all for gut checking rookies, trainees, etc. Such as have them doing 500 Hindu squats and push ups. Run them to death. But powerbombing? Come on. I guess everybody is covering up for each other. I swear for us to play sooooo tough, wrestling is made up of 90% pussies! Afraid to speak up, afraid of saying no, and afraid of getting lockerroom heat.

Well, I'm going on record right now to say to anyone remotely, allegedly, supposedly involved with that situation, you better never work with me.  In the past for no good reason, I've had an unjustified reputation for shooting on people.  I never have, honestly.  But if I ever work any of y'all, from the biggest to the smallest, I'm going to f**k you up.  From the time they play your music, 'til I pass the f**k out.  I'M GOING TO WHOOP YOUR ASSES.  I don't claim to be a bad ass, but if need be, I'm a bad motherf**ker.  Just ask any motherf**ker that has ever fought me.  I won't kill you, so this is not a death threat, but they will have a benefit wrestling show in your honor to raise money for your bills.  I really hope I've offended someone, and if I have, you can find me on Facebook, Quenton Pokerface Williams, or ask around, I'm not hard to find.  RIP Jeremy Woods, and until next time, God Bless, and keep your pimp hand strong!

**-Arena Report:  EWE Ripley, TN 9.11.10**

----Christian Jacobs with Jon Michael beat "the Ladies Man" Mark Devonci…Blaine Devine won the Ultimate Division Title  beating Seth Knight and Rockin Randy…Drew Haskins beat Nick Iggy…Johnny Bandana with Drew Haskins beat Ryan Genesis….Chase Stevens beat "The King" Shane Williams to retain the SAW Title.

For full report and notes go to:  *Yearbook 2010 Web Companion*

**-Cheap Heat:  "The Slow Painful Death of the Pro Wrestling Business" by Gene Jackson.**

Ok….so despite my current lack of internet access, as promised, I've made my way to the local McDonald's to post a column because I just can't let what I saw Friday night go without reporting.  I'm gonna warn you this is as long AS HELL…but hopefully worth your time.  Everyone knows I love wrestling, but I really haven't been to a lot of shows in recent years.  So now that I have a fiance' that's willing to go with me to shows, I've intended to start back going a bit more often.  While I do enjoy a good wrestling show, I have to admit I do like to seek out a bad one every now and then just for curiosity's sake….lucky for me I'm in Alabama so BAD wrestling shows are NOT AT ALL hard to find.  The last time Rosey and I went to Mississippi, I noticed as we passed through a small town called Snead that there was a sign at their indoor flea market that said "WRESTLING EVERY FRIDAY NIGHT".  It was spray-painted and looked pretty poor…..that stuck in the back of my mind for a couple of months untill last Friday when we really didn't have anything planned for Friday night.  We were in the process of what we had jokingly dubbed our "white trash weekend" of going to get lottery tickets, eating at the pizza buffet, and going to K-Mart so "Flea Market Wrestling" sounded like a no brainer.  I asked Rosey if she was up for it and she said the words she'd later regret, "Sure, why not?"

So Friday night we head out to Snead and when we get there, we noticed the old painted sign was now replaced by a professional looking printed sign….so we thought that maybe this isn't gonna be as bad as we first thought…..then we went to the door.  Ticket price was $5 each…..we buy our tickets and the lady tells us to "enjoy the show". We go on in and see what has to be one of the saddest excuses I've seen for a ring in quite some time......of course, as is the standard, there's 10 kids in the ring taking bumps and bouncing off the ropes and such (this would be the height of the workrate for the evening).....the ring is in a corner of the building with walls on two sides of it.....NO CHAIRS....just homemade bleachers with 4X4s to sit on.....if I thought my ass hurt after paying $10 for us to get in....I hadn't seen anything yet. God, these things were uncomfortable. We sit down and notice that we stick out like sore thumbs.....just think every stereotype of "southern rasslin' fans" you've ever heard and these people were it....all 25 of them....from best I could tell us and maybe 4 other people weren't related to the "rasslers".

Finally, it gets to be bell time and they herd the children out of the ring and start to play the national anthem until the CD starts to skip so bad they have to stop it....yes the CD was skipping. We're off to a fantastic start. Then we're having issues with the "sound system" so the announcer/ticket lady/promoter/whatever gets a megaphone to announce with. Now there's only a couple of names I was able to understand all night but that's irrelevant. AC/DC "You shook me all night long" plays as the first two "wrestlers" make their way out to the ring. The first guy I see coming down the "aisle" is wearing a pair of hiking boots with a pair of what appears to be his mother's leopard print stretch pants on with a white t-shirt with "WHO DAT" written in black sharpie along with the number "65" on the back...his name is apparently "Sling Blade"....ok. Now HE looks like a million damn bucks compared to his partner....who looks as though he got off work at the factory and came straight to the ring wearing.......dirty tennis shoes....dirtier blue jeans.....and an Alabama Crimson Tide t-shirt that sells for $5 at Walgreens...and his name?.....THE PIMP! I s**t you not...this man was THE PIMP, and he looked like Randy Owens on crack. (We'll come back to him....it gets better). The referee looks like he just got off a short bus from "special class" as he's sporting cut off blue jeans with knee high gym socks and a sweet ass folex watch he has to hand out to the ring announcer before the match starts.

Unbeknownst to us this opening match was some kinda 6 way #1 contender's match for the "UNITED STATES TITLE" as people just randomly kept coming out....there was a little guy in biker shorts and hi-top tennis shoes named "Little D"......a kid who was painted up like Sting....I never caught his name so we just called him "Low Budget Sting"....then "You shook me all night long" plays again and apparently the "top heels" in the "company" come out with toy looking belts...one guy looked to be about 40 something, his partner looked to be about 16, and they were sporting some fresh ass 'MMA Elite' shorts that you can buy at Wal-Mart along with some tennis shoes....these guys cracked me up cause they ended up coming out like 5 or 6 times during the show and they'd get their asses handed to them, then they'd walk out again to AC/DC 2 minutes later with this hard ass swagger with their toy belts like that s**t didn't just happen....strangely despite their multiple appearences I never once was able to decipher their names, so we'll just refer to them as "the champs".

So anyway six guys end up in the ring and they just break into a melee with people suplexing folks into each other and knocking each other over......there were like 5,000 clotheslines thrown throughout the night and about 200 waist high dropkicks....I've seen MUCH better wrestling on those old Backyard Wrestling videos (and better rings). Anyways...people start randomly getting pinned til it's down to two and then's theres this convoluted finish with a chain that the ref acted like he didn't see then realized he was supposed to see so he called for the bell....just painful to watch...you could hear crickets chirping as the crowd had no idea what had just happened or why the "match" was suddenly over....which then led to a long drawn out mic...err...megaphone spiel which no one knew what the hell was being said but "Low Budget Sting" said it with about as much charisma as Dean Malenko on anti-depressants...next match.

Sooo AC/DC plays again and "The Champs" return along with "Sling Blade" and "The Pimp"...however the pimp has now put on the rest of his "gimmick" which includes a sequined cowboy hat ala Randy Savage which actually looked decent and the greatest thing I've EVER SEEN....a faded...DIRTY.....denim vest with "THE PIMP" written in magic marker and faded to where you could barely make out what it said....I swear this guy had to have had this since high school...it was so bad that it was not only good.....it was f'n awesome cause this guy was rockin' this thing...not to mention he had what looked to be a couple of 15 yr old "HOES" on his arm as he walked out.  F'N Priceless....At this point my night has been made no matter what else I see.  The skinny kid from the "champs" wrestles a kid who is wearing some tights that look like they were lifted from the Fabulous Ones in the early 80's ...black with what at one time was a red lightning bolt but now just more of a dingy orange color.....another match full of low dropkicks, botched armdrags and many...many suplexes and clotheslines.....the match ended with a big run in since almost the entire heel locker room was at ringside.

INTERMISSION- We're encouraged to go hit the "concession stand" for burgers and chicken sandwichs....no thanks....back to the "action".....We are now about to witness the "WORLD HEAVYWEIGHT TITLE MATCH"....wow, holy s**t the World Title is about to be defended at the Snead Flea Market in Alabama?  Good thing we showed up tonight...so of course "You shook me all night long" plays....AGAIN! and ALL the heels come out AGAIN..."The Pimp", "The Champs", "Sling Blade" and they lead out the World Champion...and it's easy to see why he's the World Champion....he's got wrestling boots!!!  That's right, he's sporting pro wrestling boots....leather boots that looked like Bruno Sammartino wore them in his very first professional match...but boots none-the-less....the guy looks to be about 20 years old...he has tights, a t-shirt, and an A.J. Styles-esqe hooded vest....looking very much like a twin of Brian SoFine....yes my friends, this is the champ complete with the indy standard figures inc. replica of the "big gold" WCW World Heavyweight title belt...in comparison to the rest of these guys this fella looks ready for Wrestlemania and his name is apparently the "Phoenix".  The kid showed a little charisma and was actually the first guy to acknowledge the audience and actually looked down and directed a comment at me...Rosey stopped me from cutting a promo on the guy which probably would have blown all the "heels" mind...lol since they hadn't worked the crowd all night...then his opponent comes out who actually also looks like a wrestler.  He has on a purple singlet...the white/black patent leather boots made famous by "Fly Boy" Chris Kilgore, and looks like Buff Bagwell's bloated older brother....we dubbed him "Fluff Bagwell".  These two had a decent little match untill....you guessed it...ANOTHER RUN IN.....the heels hit the ring and two guys made the save...a skinny guy in green/purple tights and a fat guy with suede tights and kick pads....again...apparently the better the gear...the higher up the card...good logic I guess.....I digress...this led to another megaphone spiel that went on FOREVER with no one in the crowd really knowing what the hell was going on....we did however learn that "Fluff Bagwell" is the man responsible for this abortion of a wrestling show....they are apparently setting up a match with 19 different stipulations...it was a 6 man tag I guess and somebody was gonna have to wear a dress....one was gonna have to eat dog food....I think somebody was gonna have to wrestle with an arm tied behind their back....they went back and forth on if the toy belts were on the line...it was brutal....finally, they left the ring.

The announcer tells us they would also have a show the next night in Guntersville....I asked Rosey if she wanted to go and she quickly answered, "hell no"....AC/DC "you shook me all night long" played yet again and another match started...involving the same guys in a different variation...my ass couldn't take another minute of the "bleachers", so we decided to call it a night....as we went to leave the announcer told Rosey, "don't leave ya'll are gonna miss the good match"....so apparently they planned on having a GOOD MATCH at some point but we didn't see it. Rosey got treated to me ranting all the way back to Albertville and after we got to the house about bulls**t shows like this killing the business we all love. On one hand it's funny to watch and sad at the same time, but it also makes me mad as hell to think you've got guys like poor Jeremy Wood in Arkansas who wanted more than anything to be a part of the wrestling business and will let idiots like this try to "train" them and put their life at risk...and the fact that there are SO MANY shows like this out there that more and more this is what people think pro wrestling is....and I guess in many cases they are right....this is what it has DE-volved into....any asshole who can piece together something resembling a wrestling ring can set it up and call it a "show"....I guess me going to these things even for perverse amusement and something to write about is counterproductive because I'm sure we doubled their income for the month but I just can't help going and seeing what is out there....and to help me understand the disgusted look on many people's faces when they hear the mere mention of "wrestling." It's understandable why so many people are washing their hands of wrestling and choosing not to be associated with it.

I'm sure if anyone associated with that show was to read this they'd be pissed off and think I'm an asshole for going to their show and writing this (though the likelihood of any of those folks being able to read or knowing what the internet is, is very slim) but I think if you are willing to charge people to watch bulls**t like that and call it a "wrestling show", then you deserve to be called out and made fun of....because you're killing the business and you're too ignorant to even realize it....you don't see what you're doing for what it really is. To all the real promoters out there who strive to put on good professional shows for the entertainment of the few true wrestling fans left, I applaud you.....weather the storm and hopefully wrestling will survive.....hopefully, steps will be taken at some point to help eliminate all the crap that's out there...but I seriously doubt it.

**-Jon Michael returns to wrestling.**

**-The Thompson Perspective by Brian Thompson**

It seems like I always begin one of my columns by talking about how long it has been since the previous column. Well, regardless, here is another edition of the "Thompson Perspective."

Whether this is the start of a more regular column or the last time you read anything from me for six months, only time will tell as they say.

In this edition, I want to give all of us affiliated with the wrestling business something to think about. I guess the title of this column could be "Emotion vs. Performance." It is a discussion that I have had with Brian Tramel and a few others in or around the wrestling business.

What exactly am I talking about? Well, here goes nothing!

To me, one of the lost arts of professional wrestling is emotion. I'll soon be 30-years-old. I've watched wrestling since 1986, so obviously I have seen many changes in the business. At the time I started watching, wrestling was on fire. Texas was hot with the Von Erichs and World Class Championship Wrestling. The NWA was doing massive business with Dusty Rhodes and the Four Horsemen leading the charge. The World Wrestling Federation was going nationwide with Hulk-A-Mania as a driving force. Memphis had Jerry "The King" Lawler trying to be World Heavyweight Champion. Verne Gagne's American Wrestling Association (AWA) still had some life with good, young talent like Curt Hennig. As you can see, the business was HOT!

And there was a lot of emotion involved.

The goal of a babyface was to be popular with the fans, preferably of all ages. He should kiss babies, hug grandmas and make girls drool. The heel should be much the opposite, making babies cry, grandmas curse and girls gag. What do all those analogies have in common? Emotion!

I used to watch my late uncle try to go through the TV set to get to a heel. While that was entertaining, it was also indicative of how GOOD the guys were at drawing that emotion that I'm talking about.

Where is that emotion today? It is hard to tell.

How many times have we seen opponents shake hands following a match? I've lost count. It seems like the way the business is presented today, it is more about the "performance." Hey did we have a great match?

Let's celebrate!

This thought first came to my mind after watching a Total Nonstop Action (TNA) Wrestling match between the Motor City Machineguns and Generation Me. The Machineguns, arguably one of the top two or three tag teams in the business today, have truly impressed me. They have good fan support. But, Generation Me is hardly that accomplished. The general idea was that it is two babyface teams congratulating each other on a hard fought contest. I guess that's fine, but who cares was my first thought. How about the losers being angry that they just got beat? I know a few weeks later Generation Me turned heel, but still.

For those of you who have watched the business for a while, you can remember when there were hardly any baby vs. baby scenarios. And when there were, they were special. One of the biggest of all-time certainly had to be the WrestleMania VI match between the Ultimate Warrior and Hulk Hogan. You had the two top babies in the WWF at the time battling for both the WWF and Intercontinental titles. They had a good little feud and then a hug/handshake after the match. Guess what? It meant something! Why? Because it was rarely done.

I guess I'm dogging handshakes, when in reality I really feel that the "emotion" of wanting to see guys win is gone. It is almost like, I don't care who wins I just hope they put on a great match. And while I love some great matches, I feel that sentiment is the reason we see small crowds around the country. The most recognizable organization outside WWE and TNA is certainly Ring of Honor (ROH) Wrestling. And they often have that performance style. And guess what? The big crowds aren't there. And they're not anywhere for that matter.

I had an argument about this with a guy I've known for the better part of 10 years. He's a fan but has dabbled in the business in some ways in the St. Louis scene. I told him I wasn't impressed by the things like "This is Awesome!" chants. While that's cool, I guess, it again really doesn't draw the emotion of seeing someone win or lose. He kind of disagreed but then I reminded him of how in the 1980's and 1990's you played off emotion and not performance and had bigger houses.

I equate it to going to the movies. You don't sit there watching and think, "Gee I hope the cast gives a good performance." You typically get caught up in the storyline. Yes, you know that Robert DeNiro in "real life" doesn't hate Mel Gibson. But as part of this movie, their characters are at odds and you feel it. You certainly don't see the two shake hands when the darn movie is done!

Maybe there is no going back. Maybe things are so exposed that you can't draw that emotion. I don't know that we'll ever see the heights of the 80's or 90's, but I know that emotion exists. I've seen it. I've felt it first hand.

What do you think? Let me know on the Message Board!

**-Memphis Wrestling TV – What Did We Learn in 15 Weeks??**

-Kevin White is entertaining as hell and I miss seeing him on TV every week.

-Tommy Mercer is a monster and should be signed!!

-Su Yung still needs **a lot** of work!!

-Cody Melton has turned into a damn good worker.

-Derrick King doesn't have to be on every incarnation of Memphis Wrestling.

-Brandon Baxter is a hell of an announcer.

-Kid Nikels/Eric Wayne are a good team and impressed a lot of people.

-Brian Christopher and Wolfie D can actually contribute to a TV show.  I loved the "Too Cruel" gimmick!

-Jerry Lawler still gets the top ratings on Memphis Wrestling, but...it also proves that if it is only 11,000 people.  That is kind of like being the best player on a losing team - it really doesn't matter if you don't win!

**-Su Yung debuts in FCW – WWE's developmental.  9.18.10**

**-Arena Report:  EWA Rector, AR 9.18.10**

----Lord Humongous won a Battle Royal...Midnight Cowboy beat James Arnez...Canadian Phoenix beat Big Indian Quixote..."Doc" beat Canadian Phoenix...Street Fight: Adrian Banks beat Blackjack and Youngblood...Koko Anderson & Biscuit beat Cookie St. James/Youngblood...C-Money beat Southside Brawler..."Asylum" [Pappy/Psycho] beat Tim Edwards/Suicide.

For Full Report and notes go to:  *Yearbook 2010 Web Companion*

**-Chris Jericho mentions Flash Flanagan on RAW.  9.27.10**

----During a segment before his match with Randy Orton last night, Jericho went through a list of wrestlers he has beat before, including big time WWE names such as Stone Cold and The Rock.  He even included Japanese and Mexican wrestlers names, and then starts going into the WCW roster, including all of Nash's and Hall's gimmicks individually.  He also included Flash Flanagan in his list of people he had beat.  But...wait...contrary to what Jericho said, Jericho has only worked Flanagan ONE TIME in his whole career.  LOL  It was OVW's "The Last Dance" [last show ever in Louisville Gardens] on June 27, 2001 and Jericho fell to the OVW Champion, Flash Flanagan.  Fun segment from Jericho and good to see him put over Flash, even if it was a comedy piece.

**-Arena Report: Summer-Jam 2010 Newbern, TN 9.25.10**

----Mark Devonci beat Kevin Charles...C-Money beat J-Weezy & Hardcore Yow for the High Risks Title..." SOBs" [Mark Justice/Kid] with Auburn Thunder beat "Southern Heritage" [Tommy Redneck/Shannon Lee] with Mad Money Mike to win the NBW Tag Team Titles...
Mr. Wrestling 3000 [ Stan Lee] kept his mask and defeated Jeremy Moore to win the MACW Title...Dutch Mantell beat Sarge O'Reilly..."Team MACW" [Tim Edwards/Kid Nikels/Brad Badd] beat "Team NBW" [Chris O'Neal/Eric Wayne/Seth Knight]...Chris Rocker beat Big Red to win the NBW Title in a Barbwire Match.  For Full Report and notes go to:  *Yearbook 2010 Web Companion*

SEPTEMBER PHOTOS

Top row from left: IWA sign, Blackjack and photo from Gene Jackson's article

Middle from left: C-Money flying and Dutch Mantell vs Sarge O'Reilly

Bottom Row from left: Cookie St. James, Suicide and Tim Edwards

## OCTOBER

-ASWF Rocktoberfest draws from 3,000 to 5,000 people in Batesville, AR 10.02.10. Go to : *Yearbook 2010 Web Companion* results.

-Stan Lee returns to EWE.

-Christian Jacobs wrestles "The Golden Boy" Greg Anthony in an empty arena bout.

http://www.youtube.com/watch?v=Ndb80rQP6mU will take you to part 1

-Arena Report: NEW West Memphis, AR 10.08.10

----The RoShow beat Mike Anthony…Moe Stegall beat "The Golden Boy" Greg Anthony…Chris Stryker over Byron Wilcott…Alan Steele beat Jon Allen…Dan Matthews beat Austin Lane…First Blood Elimination: Kid Nikels/Eric Wayne beat Justin Smart/Shawn Reed [***3/4]

For Full Report and notes go to: *Yearbook 2010 Web Companion*

-Jamie Jay retires.

-Albino Rhino returns to TIWF for three shows.

-"Nightmare in Newbern" draws 200 fans for Stan Lee vs Psycho main event.

-Drama at Rector, AR show as wrestlers walk out of the building.

-Memphis Wrestling draws 150+ to "Monster Bash" show with Jerry Lawler vs Frankenstein main event.

## OCTOBER PHOTOS

**Top row from left: Seth Sabor, Terrance Ward/Enforcer/Athena Eclipse and Sid Vicious powerbombing Pokerface**

**Bottom row from left: Austin Lane vs Buff Bagwell, Moe Stegall and "Monster Smash" Poster**

## NOVEMBER

-Brian Chrisopher wins Southern Heavyweight Classic Tournament.  Memphis, TN 11.04.10

-Arkansas Athletic Commission decides to NOT regulate wrestling training.

-Cody Melton debuts in NEW and Kevin Charles says farewell.  11.05.10

-"Hollywood Blondes" [Sarge O'Reilly/Brody Hawk] debut with "Hollywood" Jimmy Blaylock in EPW.

-Jerry Lawler injured and misses Monday night RAW with staph infection.

----Lawler's left knee is swollen from the knee down to the foot.  They are saying it is a possible staph infection, but actually do not know what it is.  Even though it is believed it happened at the Forrest City show, Lawler is not sure what he did to make it happen.  Doctor advised him to not do RAW because of the 10 hour flight to England.  It would be dangerous due to increasing chances of blood clots.  The high risk kept him home.

-Coach's Corner "Professionals and Amateurs" by Brian Tramel

----I would think that most reading this are probably familiar with the NCAA rules of what defines you as a professional athlete or an amateur athlete, right??  It can be a bit complicated reading the rules, but the simple way of looking at it is – if you are paid to perform for a team, then you are a professional.  If you want to be considered an amateur athlete then you must not take money, gifts, or anything considered as pay.  I could spend a whole article on my actual feelings on all these big time colleges making tons of money off of attendance, TV contracts and gimmicks off these amateur athletes, but when thinking of the NCAA rule, I thought it would be interesting if we apply this to the area wrestling promotions.  Let's say you would not be considered a professional wrestler if you have never received a paycheck from either the WWE or TNA??  What if the promoters only had to pay professional wrestlers??  Who would be the guys that got paid and what guys would be left off the payoffs??  Let's take a quick look at all the promotions and throw around some names.

-TIWF

Pros:  Motley Cruz.  Not sure if he has ever been paid by WWE or TNA, but he has worked the territory for years and was paid by major promotions during the period.

Amateurs:  Everyone else on the roster

-ASWF

Pros:  Austin Lane

Amateurs:  Everyone else including guys that have been around forever like Rik Burton and Loose Cannon.

-NEW

Pros:  Alan Steele, Eric Wayne, Kid Nikels, Dan Matthews and Kevin Charles.  [Matthews did work as an extra right??]

Amateurs:  The one notable would be Greg Anthony.  It would be hard to not pay a guy like that, but if you went by these rules, then guys like Charles would be considered ABOVE Anthony.

-NBW

Pros:  Stan Lee and Chris O'Neal

Amateurs:  Everyone else!

-EPW

Pros:  Sarge O'Reilly would have to be considered because he falls in the same category as Motley Cruz - working territories as a jobber.

Amateurs:  Everyone else!

-EWE

Pros:  Kevin Charles, Rude, Pokerface, Eric Wayne, Kid Nikels, Jon Michael, Stan Lee and Christian Jacobs.  Ike Tucker also worked AWA in the territory days.

Amateurs:  Everyone else!  Greg Anthony is also on this roster.

-Memphis Wrestling

Pros:  Derrick King, Wolfe D, Brian Christopher, Eric Wayne, Johnny Dotson and Stan Lee.

Amateurs:  Everyone else!

-MCW

Pros:  Pokerface

Amateurs:  Everyone else!  A lot of journeymen on this roster.

-IWA

Pros:  No one!!

Amateurs:  Everyone!! You would have a team like "Asylum" [Pappy/Psycho] fall in the same category as Greg Anthony.

-TFW

Pros:  No one!!

Amateurs:  Everyone!!

SAW

Pros:  Chris Michaels, Jon Michael, Casey Kage [he has worked TNA right??] and Chase Stevens.

Amateurs:  Everyone else!

USWO

Pros:  No one!!

Amateurs:  Everyone else!

----Ok, so we have the total following pros of all the promotions in the area.  Could you promote a show with just these guys??

Motley Cruz, Sarge O'Reilly, Derrick King, Wolfe D, Brian Christopher, Johnny Dotson, Eric Wayne, Stan Lee, Austin Lane, Chris O'Neal, Alan Steele, Kid Nikels, Dan Matthews, Kevin Charles, Rude, Pokerface, Jon Michael, Christian Jacobs, Ike Tucker, Chris Michaels, Casey Kage and Chase Stevens.

----Do you agree with the assessment??  Who did I leave out??  This would change wrestling in this area with promoters making more money because they would not have to pay anyone.  Or it might help some of the legit professionals make more money.

**-Mama Says It Bees That Way Sometimes "What Local Guys Would Make It In the Territory Days" by Downtown Bruno Lauer**

----This is one of my favorite columns of the year from Bruno. I talk a lot to various people saying, "Man, that guy would have made some money in the old days..." I am usually talking about TGB or the team of "Picture Perfect", but Bruno has a great list. He also goes over the list of places you could work and make REAL money. This column was prompted by the Coach's Corner "Professionals and Amateurs" column.

It is sad that there are so many guys who in my day could and would be making their living in the business. Because, let's face it - there were territories all over the country to make a living in. Amarillo/San Antonio/Dallas/Houston in Texas. Kansas City, Minneapolis, Indianapolis, and Ohio in the Mid-West. Memphis, Knoxville, Alabama, Tampa, Louisiana and Oklahoma in the south. Hawaii, Northern and Southern California, Portland, Calgary in the west. Toronto, Montreal and the Maritime in eastern Canada. Winnipeg in Central Canada, Vancouver in Canadian West, and the WWWF in the Northeast. Georgia for Ole Anderson/Paul Jones/Fred Ward. Jim Crockett in the Carolinas and East Coast Mid-Atlantic region. Baba and Inoki in Japan. That is some of them - not the complete list.

See...these are the guys who SHOULD be making a living and WOULD have been if they were around back in the DAY, but just don't have that opportunity. There is only a limited amount of spots available now and that's it! I could definitely see these guys...but not ONLY these guys, to ward off a nuclear attack on me for leaving out somebody....making it back in my era in the territories...and, for the sake of POSITIVE conversation, may I suggest Brian Tramel opens up a thread on the message board to add to my list of guys who have the tools.

I'm intentionally leaving my list small, so as not to offend anybody. I will list only 20 guys...not in any particular order...here goes...

1: Dustin Ring

2: Alan Steele

3: Eric Wayne

4: Kid Nikels

5: Austin Lane

6: Kevin White

7: Cody Melton

8: Byron Wilcott

9: Mike Anthony

10: Greg Anthony

11: Brian Thompson

12: Chuck Poe

13: Joey Lynn

14: Asylum

15: Jocephus

16: Stan Lee

17: Derrick King

18: Kevin Christian [in creative or backstage in some capacity...very sharp mind for the business]

19: Jon Allen

20: Brandon Baxter [although he DID make a living in uswa/power pro, and in world class/global, I really believe he has the talent and ability to have gone much further if the opportunity was there.]

Just my opinion, and as I said, this isn't to start an argument – it's to start a valid discussion! I'm curious as to what everybody else thinks.

Oh,and I must give honorable mentions to Terrence Ward, Oscar Barlow, Al Hall, Moe Stegall, Matt Boyce, and many others. To Hollywood Jimmy and Brian Tramel for CARING and having a passion for the industry.

-**Pokerface appears on The Jerry Springer Show.**

-**Derrick King works NEW for the first time since 2009.**

-**Dustin Starr released from WWE developmental contract.**

-**Christian Jacobs beats "The Golden Boy" Greg Anthony to win EWE Title. Ripley, TN 11.20.10**

-**Chico Mendoza beats Motley Cruz to win TIWF Title Trenton, TN 11.20.10**

-Bishop has a car wreck.

-NEW live at Charleston, MS for their first ever house show with Eric Wayne and Kid Nickels defeating Cody Melton and Justin Smart in the main event.

## NOVEMBER PHOTOS

Top row from left: Dustin Starr [by John Coffin], Christian Jacobs and Way Cool

Bottomr from left: "Hollywood Blondes" [Sarge O'Reilly/Jimmy Blaylock/Brody Hawk], Southern Heavyweight Classic poster and Terrance Ward

## DECEMBER

-Austin Lane beat Chris Stryker to win ASWF Title Tuckerman, AR.  12.04.10

-Flash Flanagan played the part of "room service" on RAW that was live from Louisville, KY.

-Man Mountain Mike dies.

-Tommy Mercer signs with TNA.

----Mercer, who has worked some dark matches with TNA and such, looks to have won a regular role as The Amazing Red's brother.  RRO would like to congratulate Mercer and hopes he has a great experience!!

-Dustin Starr returns to the area doing color commentary for NEW.

-Kid Nikels gets a look.

----Nikels was fortunate enough to be able to not only get a look from Danny Davis and Jim Corrnette, but WWE's John Laurinaitis also attended the OVW camp.

-EWE announces that the promotion will run on Thursday nights starting in January 2011.

-Freddy James passes away 12.16.10

-RRO's Thompson reflects on Garry Lawler and Man Mountain Mike

The local wrestling world has lost two good guys in recent weeks with the passing of Man Mountain Mike and Freddy "Garry Lawler" James.  I thought I would take the time to give my memories of the two men.

### Man Mountain Mike
I never got to work with Mike, but did get to watch him during his run with Bert Prentice's Ozark Mountain Wrestling/North American All-Star Wrestling promotion.  In OMW/NAASW, Mike was sort of a novelty attraction.  He was a bigger guy and while nobody would confuse him with a Ric Flair or Ricky Steamboat from a technical wrestling standpoint, he certainly was entertaining and worked well for his size.

At times he fit the roll of being Colorado Kid's sidekick in a similar vein to what the World Wrestling Federation would do with Hulk Hogan, having various sidekicks during his run there.  I certainly want to send my condolences to Mike's family and let them know that he is appreciated for the entertainment he provided to me as a teenager during the OMW/NAASW days.

**Freddy "Garry Lawler" James**

While I never personally met or worked with Mike, I did get the chance to work with Freddy on a few occasions. The first time was about three years ago at a Professional Wrestling Alliance (PWA) show run by his brother-in-law Jamie Jay. It was in Wynne, AR at the Boys and Girls Club of Cross County with around 200 fans in attendance. The main event was Jamie, "Superstar" Bill Dundee and Brandon Baxter against Freddy in his "Garry Lawler" gimmick, Johnny Morton and Scott Fury. Freddy played the Lawler gimmick up well. He had the look of a smaller Jerry Lawler, circa 1988, with crown and even a replica of the AWA World Heavyweight Title that Lawler had held around that time period.

He was always cordial to me and seemed like a nice guy. Since that show, I've run into Freddy a few times at shows and while helping Jamie Jay at the Vanndale facility he used to run PWA events earlier this year. Living in the same county, we'd also run into each other once in awhile at Wal-Mart.

Ironically, it was just a few days ago when I saw him at the Wal-Mart in Wynne. He was a little far from me and I was in a hurry, so instead of yelling at him across the store, I figured I'd say "hello" some other time. I wish I would have yelled. You just don't know when a friend, family member, or even wrestling acquaintance will no longer be around even just to say "Hi" to. I send my condolences to his family as well.

**-Arena Report: FNW Blytheville, AR 12.18.10**

----Chris O'Neal by DQ over Cody Melton...Austin Lane beat John Michael Worthington ...Christian Jacobs by DQ over "The Golden Boy" Greg Anthony...Austin Lane beat Alan Steele...Christian Jacobs/Chris O'Neal over Greg Anthony/Cody Melton ...Derrick King beat Stan Lee in the best match of the night...Stan Lee won a Battle Royal.

**Go to *Yearbook 2010 Web Companion* for full report.**

**-200 fans show up for Thursday night show at NBW. Go to *Yearbook 2010 Web Companion* for full report.**

**-EWE Plug pulled again.**

----The on and off again story continues in Ripley, TN.

----In May of this year, JC [owner of EWE building] shut down the show stating that the show was not making money. Apparently his problems were centered around some heat he had with

Derrick King and Stan Lee. In July, EWE returned as "EWE Ultimate" without either Stan Lee or Derrick King being part of the show. Lee later joined them and seemed to smooth things over with JC. This past Saturday night, Derrick King showed up at the show. JC had told King that he was not allowed or welcome at the EWE building EVER and he was highly upset. DK was not part of the show - he just sat in the crowd and watched the show. JC was extremely angry after the show and told EWE booker Jon Michael that the show was over after this upcoming Saturday night's show.

----This throws a wrench in the plan for them to run Thursdays with SAW. No more wrestling in Ripley at this point.

----Jon Michael sent in the following statement.

**Jon Michael tells the story.....**

Just wanna say, this is probably going to be the most childish and acute reason for anyone to shut a company down!

"Its a Crazy Christmas" and that it was! That was this past Saturday's title of the event in Ripley, TN! Let me explain this first, EWE Ultimate had just made a working agreement with Showtime Allstar Wrestling! The agreement was that we would be going to Thursday nights which would be a great deal for not only talent but also Showtime Allstar Wrestling because they would have three regular shows, and also for the local talent, they would get chances to work TV that some of them usually wouldn't get. With that being said, this was going to be an every week, "EVERY WEEK" TV taping for SAW. Not only would there be a Thursday show, but the other shows would benefit from this as well! With guys who are on TV working on Thursdays, they would be able to wrestle all of the local shows that they wanted to as well! It would have been a great thing for the boys, and eventually a great thing for the area! But, BUT... JC White wants to do things his way, not the way that the business is ran! I'm not running anyone down in anyway, I'm just stating what happened, and also how business should be. Now, we all know the way business should be, isn't always how it works out and more so than not, business is never done right in this day in time so here ya go!

"Its a Crazy Christmas" Saturday, December 25th! There was a one night tournament, pitting guys like Stan Lee against Kid Nickles, Eric Wayne against Tatt2, there was a special added match one time only between Eric Wayne vs Kid Nikels, and the finals of the tournament was Tatt2 against Stan Lee. Also, there was a Drug Test on the show, and was very entertaining and Kellen James last moment in EWE history will be known as Pee Face, cuz he got Pee thrown in his mouth and face! Anyways, this was the show. That is what the show was with good matches, no drama was caused, nothing happened, nothing got broke, no one stole anything no one got into shoot fights or any of that garbage.

Derrick King walked in and sat in the back row of the show to watch a match. He only came because he and his other half gave Tatt2 a ride to the show! Period. DK caused no drama, DK I would dare say and I'm just being honest, not stabbing at DK or anything but, DK I would say probably wasn't even really noticed as being there by the fans because that's how good the matches were! This show was perfectly fine, and nothing happend! AT ALL!!!

So, with that being said, JC White saw Derrick in the crowd twice I believe, and JC White spoke to Derrick King I believe, and JC White didn't make him leave the building. If it's his building, then make him leave! I am running a show. I am not going to walk out in the middle of the show and tell someone who has a ticket watching the show causing no problems at all to leave the show. Now, NOTHING was said to me the ENTIRE, EENNTTIIRREE show about Derrick being there, and to be honest, I didn't know Derrick was even coming until minutes before the show. After the show was over, nothing was said to me still, so I waited for people to leave, and some kids wanted to get pictures with me so I went out to take a couple pictures with some children, and right in the middle of that, JC White interrupts rudely and pulls me aside! JC then goes on and on about I had Derrick King come to the show, and that it was all my doing and all my fault, that I let him in, and that I let him down and JC then said that he couldn't do this anymore, and that he is shutting the show down at the first of the year! I shook his hand and walked off! I'm not arguing a cussing old man in public and especially in front of children!

SOOO, thats exactly what he'll get! The Show will be shut down at the First of the year! I'd like to thank all the guys and the boys that worked for me, from the staff to the performers Thank you for all your hard work! Don't worry, there will be more shows to come with SAW just not that building. I will go on record of saying that the guys that have worked for me, we've had some of the best matches and the best storylines/moments of the year and I would put my crew up against any crew and we were like a family back there! So, we'll see ya later, EWE Ultimate takes the dive, rest in peace, and one more thing, the people who have heat with me, you know who you are, and you know what you've done, so don't bother me, and I won't bother you but if you show up on the wrong side of the tracks, I'll be sure there's a train ready to run you over!

HAPPY NEW YEAR to all!!

Thanks goes to: Blaine Devine, Seth Knight, Rude, Christian Jacobs, Staff, Oz, Paul Adams, Jocephus, Eric Wayne, Kid Nickles, Moe Stegal, Dan Mathews, Tatt2, Stan Lee, Pokerface, Brandon Espinosa, Chase Stevens, Drew Haskins, Johnny Bandana, Ryan Genesis, Shane Williams, Randy, JR Manson, Ike Tucker, Kellen James, myself (lol), Ken Wayne, Caleb (ref), Bishop, TJ (ref) and any other talent I have failed to mention!
Special thanks to Kathy and Jerry Mount for all your help!


**-Wayne's World: "Pissing Off the Unimportant" by Eric Wayne**

If anyone truly knows me, you know the passion I share with a select few about the sport called pro wrestling. I've been in numerous arguments about what I do and had several intelligent discussions on it, as well.  I knew when I was 6 years old sitting upstairs in the Mid-South Coliseum that I wanted to be a wrestler.  The environment I was being exposed to was different than anything else I'd ever seen, and I LOVED it!  I loved everything about it and wanted to be in the middle of it all...I wanted to be the best.  That's when the journey began.

I started out as a very young kid, just travelling with my dad to different towns, but soon was brought into the "limelight" so to speak.  I got a small taste of it and never thought twice about it.  I was going to travel and wrestle and be paid to do all of it!  Yeah, right...I forgot where the industry had fallen.  No matter how hard I wished things were different and not so terrible, I was constantly reminded of it everywhere I went.

I've made my share of mistakes and learned from them as best as I could.  However, there are guys out there that continually make mistakes and piss on a business that was once considered mainstream and popular.  At one time, being a pro wrestler put you at "celebrity" status.  Wrestlers were tough and guys you didn't wanna mess with.  What's it like these days?  A joke.

I know, I know, I know...you're all saying I'm beating a dead horse, and I might be.  Maybe I'm venting my frustrations to the internet.  Maybe, just maybe, I'm trying to make a difference.  I hear all the time that guys wish things were like they used to be...as they sit there with beer bellies hanging over their oleather shorts and they pull their knee pads down and stuff them inside the kickpads they wore a few minutes ago during the abortion of a match they just had.  Did I mention it only went 7 minutes and they're complaining about being blown up??  Because that is the state of wrestling today.  Book a card in a town with nothing better to do than watch a bunch of losers pretend they're on the "grandest stage of them all!!"

It doesn't have to be the wrestlers without gear or talent that are tearing this business apart either.  It's the company owners and bookers.  It does not matter if you're an old man that has a grudge against one person and you shut the company down.  It does not matter if your dad bought a company for you to pretend you're Randy Orton and let everyone else run your show but YOU.  It does not matter if you wrestle under a mask even though everyone knows your identity and that you own the company.  Or that you won't pay the talent what they deserve, but think it's perfectly ok to book yourself in the last match (NOT the main event) just because you're a mark either.  What it all boils down to is this:  a whole boatload of idiots that outnumber the business-minded PROFESSIONALS left in a dying industry.

A lot of you that are reading this are probably wanting to write BT with your very own one-hit column to knock me.  But I'd rather you do it to my face.  We're all in a sport that calls itself the king of kings, which means we're all men, right?  Then why do we all act like little boys?  Whether it's a childlike state of mind or just not understanding that to be an athlete you should train, perform and look like one, not to mention act like one.  In a business that isn't a HOBBY and intended to make money, why do so many people think they can wear street clothes, carry a broom and call themselves "smart"?  Why is it that they can be 150lbs of skin and bones, or have a flabby, gross, never-been-in-a-gym body or carry 250lbs of fat and puke but wonder why the small crowd laughs at them?  Why do people think they can book their show TWO hours before belltime or start 20 minutes late or do any of the stupid things they do?  Because they're in the business.  Wait-no.  They're killing what's left!  So to all the people that know I'm talking about them, it's nothing personal against you...it's just your less than half-assed involvement and lack of dedication or heart that pisses me off.

**-'Twas the Night Before the New Year.**

----Due to being "under the weather" and just forgetting to post this year's "Twas the Night Before Christmas," I present to you a slightly different version of our annual poem.

**'TWAS THE NIGHT BEFORE THE NEW YEAR**

'Twas the night before the New Year, and low the house
Jon Michael was smiling big and it was after the day of Klaus
In the dressing rooms, the workers were talking Wrestler of the Year
Hoping they could wrestle and then go get a beer

The fans were marking out of their heads
Waiting to hear what TGB said
Out from the back came John Steele
Who swore "I don't want to be nominated!!  What is my deal??!"

In the parking lot, arose such a mass
It was Derrick King from RRO Awards past
Standing by the window, it was his friend CJ
King yelled, "You know you can call him Viper or Girl Candaay"

As I looked outside again at the new-fallen snow
Title belts mean nothing, you know??
When, what to my wondering eyes should appear
But a black man with blond hair holding a beer
He was so lively and wearing a crown on loan
His chest pushed out and he said, "It is the weekend, you know."

Now PP!! Now Tatt2!! Now LSD!! Now Austin Lane!!
On Asylum!! On Seth Knight!! On Downtown Bruno!! On Ken Wayne!!
To the dressing room!! To the ring!! To the mat!!
Now hiptoss!! Now bodyslam!! Now rat!!

As the man made himself the center of the show
The fans were chanting " Go, Stan, Go!!"
He yelled at the fans and said go home
I would rather be here all alone!!

He was dressed all in wrestling gear, from his head to his foot
And his gear was all tarnished with vodka and soot
His crown almost falling off the top of his head
"I will be the KING!!", he proclaimed, only when Lawler is dead

His eyes—they were so blurry!!  His speech so slurred!
His cheeks were red as cherry!!  His vision was blurred!!
His mouth drooled like a sleeping bear
"Do you know who I am??  3 time Wrestler of the Year!!"

The straw of his drink he held tight in his teeth
And smoke encircled his head like a wreath
Cody Melton was here for the night
He yelled, "JC, not me, killed Ripley, that is just not right!!"

He was colored and blond, a right grumpy man
And I laughed when he said he was the best in the land
A wink in his eye, a twist of his head
Wrestling in Mississippi again, oh I dread

He sprang out of the ring, to his crew gave a whistle
And away the workers flew behind him like the down of a thistle
But I heard him exclaim, as his girlfriend drove him out of site
"Happy New Year to all, and I am Derrick King....DAMMIT!!"

## DECMBER PHOTOS

**Top row from left: Shawn Reed, Downtown Bruno and Adrian Banks**

**Bottom from left: Alan Steele, Jon Michael/Derrick King and Chris Stryker**

## TOP 20 SHOWS OF 2010

Go to

for the *Yearbook 2010 Web Companion* for complete results and stories on the shows.

----The first 17 shows are listed based purely on attendance with the last three added for their importance. All our listed in ordered of the number of fans that attended. "4ᵗʰ in the Forest" and "Rocktoberfest" were the two top shows for the last three shows. Greg Anthony, Alan Steele and Brian Christopher appeared on more shows than anyone with 7 appearances. Jerry Lawler appeared on 6 shows.

20: RCW Forrest City, AR 6.19.10 Attendance: 80 "The Golden Boy" Greg Anthony defeated Kid Nikels…"All That" Alan Steele defeated "Dynamite" Seth Knight…- Premiere Brutality ("3G" Eric Wayne & Kid Nikels) defeated Midnight Gold ("Beautiful" Bobby Eaton & "The Golden Boy" Greg Anthony)… Ron Rage defeated Matt Riviera… Jon Michael Worthington defeated Christian Jacobs to become the first ever RCW Champion.

19: NEW "Scars & Stripes" West Memphis, AR 7.02.10 Attendance: 80-100 Blaine Devine beat Jon Allen by DQ… Kid Nikels beat Jeremy Moore… Shawn Reed/Justin Smart beat "Prime Danger" [Kevin Charles/Dan Matthews]…. Moe Stegall beat Alan Steele… Austin Lane beat Eric Wayne to win the US Title match.

18: NEW 2cnd Anniversary Show West Memphis, AR 10.08.10 Attendance: 125+ The RoShow beat Mike Anthony…Moe Stegall beat "The Golden Boy" Greg Anthony…Chris Stryker over Byron Wilcott…Alan Steele beat Jon Allen…Dan Matthews beat Austin Lane…First Blood Elimination: Kid Nikels/Eric Wayne beat Justin Smart/Shawn Reed.

17: NBW Summer-Jam Newbern, TN 9.25.10 Attendance: 170+ Mark Devonci beat Kevin Charles…C-Money beat J-Weezy & Hardcore Yow for the High Risks Title…" SOBs" [Mark Justice/Kid] with Auburn Thunder beat "Southern Heritage" [Tommy Redneck/Shannon Lee] with Mad Money Mike to win the NBW Tag Team Titles…Mr. Wrestling 3000 [ Stan Lee] kept his mask and defeated Jeremy Moore to win the MACW Title…Dutch Mantell beat Sarge O'Reilly…"Team MACW" [Tim Edwards/Kid Nikels/Brad Badd]

16: TIWF "November Pain" Trenton, TN 11.06.10 Attendance: 229 Geno Sydal def. Big Brad Simpson…Pretty Boy James def. Cletus Y. Tittle…Psycho def. Bumblebee of "The Hive"…Geno Sydal def. Pretty Boy James to win the vacant TV Title…Knockout Kid def. Taylor Payne…Million $$ Baby def. Black Widow© to win the women's title…Way Cool def. Motley Cruz© in a non-title match…Chico Mendoza def. Albino Rhino …Hard Justice© def. Hero Killers to retain the Tag Team Titles

15: New Blood Wrestling "Vendetta" Newbern, TN 2.06.10 Attendance: 270+ Shannon Lee beat J.Weezy… Tim Davis/Big Daddy LaFonce/KoKo Anderson def. The Mo. Badd Boys/Void… The Kid/Kid J def. Ron Rage/Lil Devil… Mark Justice def. Lord Humongous…Jason Reed/Chris Rocker def. Syn/Stunner… Crazy Train def. Motley Cruz… The Family of Pain ( Sarge/Mickey Ray) def. Jeremy Moore/Sid Vicious.

14: TCW Pine Bluff, AR 6.12.10 Attendance: 300  Tim Storm (with Apoc) pinned Action Jackson…"Golden Boy" Greg Anthony beat Wes Robinson… Jeff Jett beat "All That" Alan Steele (with Rich Rude)… "Hacksaw" Jim Duggan pinned Prince Al Farat… Athena pinned Malia Hosaka… Lethal Romance (Matt Riviera & Jay Lethal) beat Tag Team Champions The Dark Circle (Tim Storm & Apoc)… D-Lo Brown (with D'Angelo Dinero) pinned Mr. Anderson

13: Mid-South Wrestling Ft. Smith, AR 1.16.10 Attendance: 400  Dexter Hardway with Talon beat Shawn Shultz with Tony Laccassio… Prince Al Farat beat Private Sebren… John Saxon beat Prince Al Farat… Apoc defeated Wes Robinson… Steve Anthony beat Greg Anthony with Brian Thompson via disqualification… Athena beat Malia Hosaka… Tim Storm beat Al Snow… Reckage & Romance (Matt Riviera & Jeff Jett) beat Alan Steele & Buddy Landel

12: Memphis Championship Wrestling Boliver, TN 3.19.10 Attendance 400+ Patrick Smith beat Mr. Wrestling #4…"Genocide" [Albino Rhino/Maxx Corbin] defeated "Picture Perfect" [Christian Jacobs and Jon Michaels]…Koko B Ware beat Doug Heximer…Spellbinder beat Bones & Black Ice in a handicap match…Brian Christopher & Doug Gilbert defeated Derrick King & Cody Melton…Jerry Lawler over Kevin White w/ Garry White…Spellbinder wins the 12 man over the top rope battle royal to become the first ever Tennessee Battle Royal Champion.

11: HCW Jackson, TN 5.07.10 Attendance: 400+  Albino Rhino beat Christian Shane… Bones and Black Ice defeated Rude and Patrick Smith…Cody Melton beat Greg Anthony…Maxx Corbin beat Christian Jacobs…Spellbinder beat Derrick King… Brian Christopher and Mr. Catlett beat Nature Boy Kevin White and Mr. Heximer.

10: ASWF "Payback" Tuckerman, AR 5.09.10 Attendance: 400+ Loose Cannon vs. Christopher Lee… Reggie Montgomery vs. Chris Stryker… Hot Rod John Ellison vs. Lee Michaels… Su Yung vs. Nikki Lane… Mike Anthony vs. Seth Sabor… Johnny Hawk/Wild Bill vs. Morgan Williams/ "The Sexay Assassin" [Brian Christopher]… Cason McClain vs. Austin Lane vs. Cody Murdoch… Demon X with Hollywood Jimmy/Su Yung vs. Jerry The King Lawler

9: ASWF "Christmas with The King" Tuckerman, AR 12.18.10 400 "White Chocolate" Athena Eclipse defeated Big Al and Loose Cannon to retain the Euro Title….Seth Sabor retained the X Division Title over Mike Anthony, Jon Allen, and Lee Michaels in a Fatal Four Way….Johnny Hawk & Hot Rod Elision defeated Cowboy Chris Frazier & his mystery partner Mike Anthony….Austin Lane defeated Brian Christopher to retain the ASWF Championship…."CCR" [Demon X/Wild Bill] defeated Bonecrusher & Cassanova Kid to capture the Tri State Tag

Titles….In the Main Event Jerry The King Lawler defeated Outlaw Don Bass.

8:  Traditional Championship Wrestling Russellville, AR 1.23.10 Attendance: 500 Apoc pinned Steve Anthony… Prince Al Farat beat Scott Murdoch… Kid J beat Lil' Bruiser… Johnny Dotson beat Alan Steele with Rich Rude… Reckage & Romance (Matt Riviera & Jeff Jett) beat Midnight Gold (Bobby Eaton & Greg Anthony) with Brian Thompson… Tim Storm beat Al Snow

7: MCW Luxcora, AR 3.16.10 Attendance: 517 Jeremy Spiker beat Ray…Pimp/Southside Brawler beat VMan/Officer Hudson…Frankie Tucker/Homer Lee by DQ over Hambones…Nay Nay by DQ over Ms Candy…Pokerface beat Frankie Tucker.

6:  JLMW Delta Fair Memphis, TN 9.05.10 Attendance: 632 Johnny Dotson beat Albino Rhino with Hollywood Jimmy Blaylock…Kevin White with Garry White beat Jocephus…Eric Wayne/Kid Nikels beat "Too Cruel" [Wolfie D/Brian Christopher]… Jerry Lawler beat Reggie B Fine with Hollywood Jimmy Blaylock.

5:  CWA "Night of Legends" Savannah, TN 2.13.10 Attendance: 700 Chris Lexus beat Bloodbath…Destiny beat BB…South Fight Club beat Danny Morris/David Andrews…Johnny Morton beat Don Bass with "Gentleman" Jim Casey…Bill Dundee beat Max Steel…Jerry Lawler beat Buff Bagwell

4:  CWA "Night of Legends" Ripley, MS 2.12.10 Attendance: 700 to 1000   Max Steel beat Chris Lexus…Destiny vs Su Yung – No contest…Jeff Daniels beat Gary Valiant…Johnny Morton beat Don Bass with "Gentleman" Jim Casey…Dutch Mantell/Max Steel beat Bill Dundee/Marc Anthony…Jerry Lawler with Grady Watson beat Buff Bagwell with Jimmy Blaylock/Su Yung

3:  SAW "Unfinished Business" Nashville, TN 2.13.10 Attendance: 1000+  Ryan Genesis defeated Big Bully Douglas…Kevin White w/Su Yung defeated Cody Melton…Brian Christopher defeated Sigmon…Chase Stevens defeated David Young w/Paul Adams…PG-13 (Wolfie D/J.C. Ice) defeated Derrick King Enterprises (Derrick King/JT Stahr w/Sista O"Teelyah & Drew Haskins) to win the SAW Tag Team Championship…SAW Women's Champion Tracy Taylor defeated Sue Yung in to retain…Hammerjack vs. Marc Anthony ended in a no contest ruling…Andy Douglas defeated Jesse Emerson…Vordell Walker defeated Drew Haskins w/Sista O'Feelyah by DQ…Micah Taylor defeated Sigmon…Flash Flanagan defeated Rick Santel by DQ…Chase Stevens defeated Kid Kash to become the SAW International Champion.

2:  RCW "Fourth in the Forest" Jonesboro, AR 7.04.10 Attendance: 3000  Seth Knight defeated Chris O'Neal and Stan Lee… Rodney Mack & "All That" Alan Steele defeated Jamie Jay & Tony Gunn… Derrick King, Christian Jacobs and Cody Melton defeated Jon Michael Worthington, Bobby Eaton and "The Golden Boy" Greg Anthony.

1: ASWF Tuckerman, AR Rocktoberfest Batesville, AR 10.02.10 Attendance: 3000+ Seth Sabor defeated Jocephus with "Dirty" Dutch Mantel... Lee Michaels & "The Birdman" Koko B. Ware defeated "Hot Rod" John Ellison & Johnny Hawk... Money Inc's Enforcer with Commissioner T-Bone Terrence Ward & Athena Eclipse defeated Mark Marshall... The Nasty Boys (Brian Knobbs & Jerry Sags) with "The Mouth of The South" Jimmy Hart defeated CCR "Crazed Country Rebels" Demon X & Wild Bill with "Hollywood" Jimmy Blaylock... Loose Cannon & Sid Vicious defeated Pokerface & Lord Humongous.. "The Stryking Image" Chris Stryker & Mike Anthony defeated "Grandmasta Sexay" Brian Christopher & Reggie B. Fine... Buff "The Stuff" Bagwell defeated "The Human Highlight Reel" Austin Lane... The Steiner Brothers (Rick & Scott) defeated Casino & Reggie Montgomery with Commissioner T-Bone Terrence Ward & Athena Eclipse in their corner-Special Guest Referee was Terry Funk

## TOP 10 STORIES OF 2010

10: Tommy Mercer and Su Yung sign deals with TNA and WWE respectively.

9: Jerry Lawler files lawsuit against Corey Maclin.

8: EWE and DoggCW both close doors - two of the most successful area promotions.

7: Jeremy Moore buys MACW and owns all of Dyersburg.

6: RRO Tag Team 2009, MVP Team 2009 and RRO Hall of Fame member Bobby Eaton spends time in the hospital and decides to do personal appearances only due to health.

5: RCW and ASWF both get local TV on Channel 8. Both shows were canceled.

4: Memphis Wrestling returns to TV for 15 weeks.

3: NEW debuts on TV 50 in Mississippi in February and stays on the air all year long.

2: RRO Wrestler of the Year 2009 Dustin Starr signs with WWE/FCW. He works 6 months and is released.

# 1: Jeremy Wood's death.

## -RRO announced a new feature for 2010 – *Conversation*. Here are some highlights.

**-Jon Michaels talks about his health and supplements.**

*----Ok, first of all Jon Michael, give us an update on your health.*

I had a doctor follow up last Wednesday. I am cleared to drive. I can not wrestle at this moment. The doctor said that it will take some time for me to rebuild strength, stamina, and my system back up, but that with time I should recoup! I was told that the ruling of a seizure was probably a wrong ruling. He said that what I had was a very serious severe chemical reaction to things I was putting into my body. The mix of coffee, workout supplements, and energy drinks ended up being too much for my body to process. It shut me down, put my body into shock and convulsions and was a very bad reaction! Worse than a seizure because I was conscious. It was more severe because I was trying to fight out of it. In a seizure he said you tend to not be able to do much afterwards, and most of the time you are passed out!

*----So this was all caused by workout supplements and the mixing of stuff??*

A message to the boys would be if you're drinking energy drinks, stop it. If you are taking supplements, pay attention to what you are putting in your body, and listen to your body! Don't think you are superman like I did, and think that you can just go do shows, work out, not sleep, drink, work out and take supplements and energy drinks and be fine! Not true. I was already aware of my health when this happened. If you are not taking care of yourself, then do so now. Because trust me, you do not want to find yourself in a mess of your own blood, cut and bruised with blood all over your face and not being able to move thinking you are dead! I'm not exaggerating in the slightest bit!

*----What ingredients did he caution you about in the supplements??*

He didn't give a certain ingredient per say. He said that any time you put something in your body, there will be side effects, whether they be good or bad. He said the mix of the caffeine, energy drinks, and workout supplements are something that he has been seeing a lot of this year.

He said I'm 27 years old, and I'm in good health, and that I can't be doing all of that stuff. He also said that half of it was uncalled for. Also, he said that it is far more beneficial to your body, and that you would be amazed at the results you can get naturally!

**For full interview go to http://rasslinriotnews.blogspot.com/2010/07/wednesday-conversation-with-jon-michael.html**

**-Maxx Corbin talks about Randy Byrd.**

**-You had an incident recently with Randy Byrd aka Ravishing Randy where he tripped you in the crowd?? What happened??**

I'm sure he thought I'd go right to the boards or something and give him and his company some publicity, but the fact that this happened about a month ago and only a few people know about it put that to rest…lol. To be honest I don't know what his motivation was for it, but it happened.

I was in Ripley and going over some stuff with my opponent when I walked back to the main area of the locker room. That's when I saw him shaking hands with people in the back. It was like in the movies when you see a bunch of people dancing and the camera splits them all slowly until you see the main focus. He noticed me about 5 seconds after I saw him, and he looked right at me kinda nervously, and quickly went back to his guys at the other side of the room. I thought it was weird. I mean, I have been very vocal about how he was a nobody in our business and that "running" a company for 25 or 30 years (whatever the number is) that is neither well known nor respected by anyone, means nothing. I also said that they worked their attendance numbers because 1: I saw them do it when we were in the company. And 2: I witnessed it when they were coming on our local access (and no I did not watch your shows, but when you post that you had 300 people there I checked to see. Most of the time, I could only count 50 at the max.).

But in all of that I never made any violent threats toward the guy. In fact it had been a LONG, LONG time since I had mentioned him. So, I went to Jon Michael to see why he was even here. Had he been invited? The 2 guys he came with (Kilo, who I don't have a problem with, and Devon Day, who I don't know and also don't have a problem with) had been invited but apparently not him.

Anyway, they go sit in the crowd to watch the show. I had a great match against TGB, btw…lol. After my match, Jon Michael told me that he needed me to go out and celebrate with Seth Knight after he won the tournament for the ultimate title. At the end of the show you always have people starting to file out of the building. So, I walk to the ring, holding a bottle of sparkling grape juice, and I have to pass right in front of Randy (who is in the middle of the aisle walking out of the building). As I pass him, he kicks the back of my heel. The kick was heavy enough that I knew it wasn't considered an accident. I stopped and turned around to see him almost out of the building…it wasn't my moment, it was Seth's. I did send Caleb (the ref) to the back to tell JM that (in my exact words) "IF THAT FAT CLETUS T JUDD F**K TOUCHES ME AGAIN, HE'S GOT PROBLEMS."

So, we finished the deal and I got to the back. JM asks me what happened and I told him, there was also about 2 others who saw it happen, and they said the same thing I did…he tried to trip me…Was this high school? Someone then mentioned that he was in the back. I walked over and yelled, "RANDY! WHAT THE F**K WAS THAT?" He started stuttering out some excuse and walking towards me. At that point I told him that it was best he stay out of my face. I went to get dressed and he stayed on the opposite side of the room. He was trying to politic anyone he could to come work for him in Trenton…which made me laugh. As I'm putting on my clothes Randy comes up to me and asks if I have a problem with him. I noticed that most of the boys had left the room except for his Kilo and Seth. I told him that he needed to get out of my face. He then told me that he thought this had something to do with the beef we had in the past.

My reply was "THIS IS ABOUT YOU TRYING TO F**KING TRIP ME OUT THERE! NOW GET OUT OF MY FACE!"

This drew a bit of attention and some of the boys were coming back into the locker room. Randy bends down almost whispering in my ear and says "I don't respect you." It was said so low and with a lack of confidence usually reserved for a 13 year old dork that's trying to ask out the head cheerleader. So, I replied with the natural response of "WHAT!??!" I was thinking that is the dumbest thing anyone has ever said to me. Not that it made me mad, or that I couldn't hear it; it was just so random and stupid. Was he gonna tell me his dad could beat up my dad next? So, he thinks I didn't hear so he repeats himself, "I don't respect you." with the same delivery as before. My response was, "Then why the f**k are you even talking to me then Randy?" I was waiting on him to be stupid and slap me or something, but after he stuttered around talking I realized he was just wasting my time. I finally just looked at him and told him to just get the f**k out. I guess he caught on that I meant business because he walked out the door. I explained to those around that I was actually surprised that he even came up to me and said anything. Randy was good at pussying out when it came to that stuff. That was when one of his guys chimed in with, "You know why he did that right?" "It's cause ya'll were here," I said, "and he thought you'd jump in if I did anything." He said I was right and that, "Randy was a pussy." I swear to God I laughed when I heard that. So it's not only me that thinks it, huh?. Anyways, I'm not sure what it was over or what the objective was. All I know is that it was the most pathetic attempt at picking a fight I have ever seen. I was commended later for holding my cool, but in all seriousness it was more sad than threatening.

**For Full interview go to: http://rasslinriotnews.blogspot.com/2010/08/new-regular-feature-wednesday.html**

**-Kevin White talks Jeremy Wood and trainees.**

**-Give us your thoughts on the Jeremy Wood incident.**

This should never have happened. Training to become a professional wrestler is a long slow process! It is no different than lawyers/doctors/teachers going to collegee. They would not get a degree from Bubba down the street! They attend a credible school in order to learn everything neccesary to own their craft. That so called wrestling school is not a school. It sounds like they just take people's money, then abuse them for their own enjoyment! If you are going to a wrestling school and all they do is beat on you, RUN RUN RUN. There are good schools out there in all areas of the country for young guys to learn the right way. (Our School, Ken Wayne's School,

Handsome Jimmy Valiant, Harley Race, Wild Somoans, Knox pro, Danny Davis, etc)  Find the school that you feel most comfortable with.  I really feel bad for this guy's family.  I am a father and I feel it is my job to protect my kids, so I can only imagine how they feel.  The people should be held responsible!!  We have never injured anyone at our school, and we pride ourselves on that.  Now you will have bumps, bruises and an occasional mat burn, but that should be the extent of it.  I hope this death can send out a message to everyone wanting to get into pro wrestling.  Make sure you attend the right school and do your homework on the school before attending.  If you have never heard of the trainer, or never seen him on TV, don't go to that school!

**-You have a few trainees that are working on a regular basis.  Give us your thoughts on each one of these -**

**-Su Yung?**  Drove across the country straight to the school, paid her money, and never looked back!  She is very dedicated and knows what she wants out of this profession.  She set her goals and acheived them.  Most importantly, she realizes that once she arrives in Florida, it will be like starting all over and she will have to work twice as hard.  I wish her the best, she desrves everything she has received.

**-Cody Melton?**  Eats, sleeps, and breathes wrestling!!  He is willing to drive all over the US for a match or an opportunity!  Has made mistakes, but most importantly he has learned from each mistake, which has made him a better wrestler.  Also understands that he has to work every day to improve.

**-Maxx Corbin?**  Nice guy, sometimes too nice!  He could actually accomplish so much more in this business if he set his mind to doing so.  He has always been a team player and I would love to see him get an opportunity really soon to step up and let loose!

http://rasslinriotnews.blogspot.com/2010/09/wednesday-conversation-with-kevin-white.html

**-Lauren Jenkins talks about butt grabbing and being from outside the business.**

**-I got to hear the story about the butt grabbing.  Give us the lowdown.  Who was it that did it?  And you responded by "back handing" the guy??**

It can get kind of intimidating in the ring sometimes.  Those guys are pretty big, athletic, and I have felt I was about to get bounced out of the ring a couple of times (that could be fun) while preparing for the camera to roll.  The instance you are referring to was when I was in the ring with Wolfie D and Brian C and someone grabbed me right there on my booty.  Instinctively, without looking, I back handed Wolfie D right on his chest (I'm sure it hurt...not!).  The cameras weren't on me so no one even saw it.  Wolffie D started whispering something intimidating in my ear and at the time I didn't realize he was joking with me so...yes, I was getting nervous.  Later on, shortly after Brian C playfully asked me to sit on his lap next to the announcers table, I went up to Wolfie D and apologized.  He told me he was just joking around with me.  Those guys have always been pretty playful towards me on the show (dancing around, etc.) and this was another instance. They're hilarious anyway and and have quite the camera presence.

**You would be considered a person "outside" the wrestling business getting a job "inside" this world. Have you met any resistance?**

You know, I really haven't met any resistance. Everyone at the show and all the audience members have been really great towards me. Of course there are some critics out there that compare me to more experienced announcers and aren't fans, but that's always going to happen. I don't think the critics really get to see the whole picture and understand what I'm up against. But each time I learn more and more and hopefully keep getting better. I am serious about it and at some point would love to have a part in an expanded story line somehow.

**For the full interview go to http://rasslinriotnews.blogspot.com/2010/09/wednesday-conversation-with-lauren.html**

**-Derrick King talks about area promotions and RRO's Top 10 2009.**

**-You have worked almost every promotion in this area, but have recently been working mostly in the Nashville area. I am going to name three promotions, and we know there are various reasons you are not working there, but just give your opinions.**

They will all say my drinking lol lmao.

NBW - Could be a good company, Jeremy has a sliiiiight ego, lol, bigger than mine, lmao. I just think the show is designed to make him look good. He was more concerned with putting out the Walkers, which was not too hard. There is a lack of respect for talent on his show. You gotta pay the guys and you gotta put guys with talent out there. Booking Buckwheat for 5 bucks is A. not fair and B. Buckwheat should not be wrestling. Too much family involved, not enough wrestling people involved.

EWE - Management has too much say - Mr. JC should be gone. Jon Michael is doing his best with what he has to deal with. At one time Ripley was the place to be, but now I think it is so tainted and watered down.

NEW - Cool concept, I think they have some of the best talent in the area working there, but just no place to showcase them.

**-You have stated "off the record" to me before that you at times feel this site hurts the area. Do you think the site has been good or bad for wrestling in this area?? And remember, you are three time RRO wrestler of the year. LOL**

Lol, I really don't read the site much anymore, but I see everyone has a column now. Wow! That's wild! Lol. I, however, do think the site gives guys exposure and shines a light on what's going on in this area, good or bad.

**-Not sure if we have you enough heat yet...lol...so I am going to put the RRO Top 10 from 2009 here and you can say a few words about each guy.**

10: Kevin White- Cool guy, easy to work with. I think Kevin likes to wrestle closer to home, and would have been a shoe in for one of the top 80's wrestlers, which he grew up on.

9: Eric Wayne - I think he is a product of a 3rd generation wrestling family with some shoes to fill, which leads to his heat with some of the boys. I think he has a lot of pressure on him. I've heard that he could be a bit stiff or careless in the ring, never has happened with me. My advice would be to make it look real without hurting your opponent.

8: Alan Steele - Hands down one of the best guys I've ever been in the ring with. Should have a job somewhere. I don't think he likes playing politics.

7: Greg Anthony - Another hands down one of the best guys I've ever wrestled. He knows his s**t inside and out; he could do this in his sleep. One of those guys you go to the ring with and never say a word and just go.

6: Stan Lee - My brother, what bad can I say about him? Lol, very athletic and could take any bump and make it look like he is dead which is awesome. I wish he wrestled full-time; he is that good.

5: Pokerface- Have not seen him in a while, but he knows his craft and is all business in the ring. Wish we worked on more shows together.

4: Rodney Mack - Good look, works hard - no reason why he shouldn't be in WWE or TNA.

3: Derrick King - Drinking or no drinking, I love and have a super strong passion for the wrestling business. I will do anything to have a good show - love to entertain.

2: Dustin Starr -Need I say more? He has a deal. He did what it took to get there, and he deserves to be there. A good friend and I couldn't be happier for him. Always fun on the road with him - I miss him.

1: Austin Lane - Fun guy to work - loves high spots, lol, which is not all that bad. Lmao. Great guy - loved our angle in ASWF. I wish he would get out of Arkansas and be seen more places. Always a plus to a show.

http://rasslinriotnews.blogspot.com/2010/09/wednesday-conversation-with-derrick.html

-Dutch Mantell talks advice and Sarge O'Reilly.

**-Advice you might give a young wrestler reading this site??**

If you really want to advance in the world of pro wrestling, be prepared to become a serious student of the game. Be trained by someone reputable...and someone who has been there before. If you're trained by someone who hasn't been either to WWE or WCW, or at least worked 10 or 15 years in the ring, then you're wasting your money. Don't fool yourself...to be a success in pro wrestling is more than just doing a couple of good moves.

**-You have been doing some local shows, such as USWO for Tony Falk and some Legends shows. How does it feel to be back on the road again? Are the fans different this time out, or do most of them remember Dutch Mantell??**

On the Legends shows, yes, all of them know the Dirty Dutchman. I've done Legends shows in several states and am doing one in New Jersey in October thanks to the YouTube videos. It feels good to be out again...and didn't know I missed it until I got back out there.

**-You have a wrestling school now, so give us the details on that. Also, Jocephus is the guy most people are referring to "Dutch Mantell's student." What are your thoughts on him and his future??**

The school is called the University of Dutch, located about 20 minutes outside Nashville. This school is probably the best equipped training facility in the South, and if anybody is serious about training to be a pro wrestler, this is the place for you. There's a helluva lot more to the pro wrestling business than just wrestling, and what I teach at my school is the whole package. Jocephus has come a long way in a short amount of time, and I expect him to advance at a quick pace.

**-Saturday night you will be in Newbern, TN to wrestle Sarge O'Reilly. O'Reilly was well known as a Memphis TV jobber "in the day", but has made a pretty good career working the promotions in this area. For the new people around the business, how important was the role that O'Reilly played in getting over say Dutch Mantell?**

The role that Sarge played was very important, and it couldn't be done without talent like him. But when Memphis Wrestling was in its heyday, it was more or less left to the individual to get his own character over. Memphis, at the height of its popularity, was the BEST WRESTLING SHOW on TV. Bar none. Better than WWF, better than WCW, and better than all the rest of them. When you worked in Memphis, your role was to sell tickets and get people to watch. There were no classes given, no interviews written out in advance for you and no agents to walk you through things. We did it on our own talent. We did Memphis TV in 2 and a half hours...and 90 minutes of that was the LIVE SHOW. It takes 14 hours to do a RAW. What people don't truly understand is that we wrestled in Memphis 52 weeks a year. And for most of the time that I was in Memphis, we averaged 6 to 10 thousand fans per week. Imagine if WWE came to Memphis every week for a year...they would sell out 12.000 seats the first time, 6 thousand the second time, 3 thousand maybe the 3rd time and then....down to 800 people and then they'd be gone. Guys...when we used to do it....it was an art and not just anybody could do it.

**For Full interview go to: http://rasslinriotnews.blogspot.com/2010/09/wednesday-conversation-with-dutch.html**

**-Dowtown Bruno talks about working for the WWE.**

A day in my life at WWE consists of leaving Mississippi the day before the event, whether I'm flying to a far location such as the west coast or up north or whatever, or driving to a not so distant place such as Ohio or Texas. The reason for this is that I am very dedicated and professional. As I have been wherever I've worked, and I would rather be there unwinding the night before safe and secure, rather than risk a travel dilemma (canceled flight, traffic problem, etc...) the day I'm supposed to be there. Anyway, I arrive at the arena around noon and I am there until the last televised match is over, so usually I put in 10 or 11 hour days.

**For Full interview go to: http://rasslinriotnews.blogspot.com/2010/09/wednesday-conversation-with-downtown.html**

**-Brian Tramel talks about Hollywood Jimmy, stars and Mississippi wrestling.**

**-What the hell is Blaylock doing on that site?? Do I have to look at pictures of Psycho all the time??**

I have been asked this by a few people. Jimmy seems to have decided to do the site by upholding all the storylines and such. He works for EPW and various other promotions. He wants to keep the illusion alive. That keeps him in good graces with everyone in dressing rooms and such. I have no problem with it, and he might actually get more people coming to the site because of it.

I personally designed this site to be a "smart" site for the workers and fans in this area. I modeled it after the Wrestling Observer Newsletter with no big graphics – no bells & whistles – just opinion and news. When I post results, we do post them from the point of view that the fans saw that night. When I do my Arena Reports, I never pretend something is legit, when it is not.

I also feel I could get more hits if I actually did "copy and paste" stuff from other areas, but I wanted to pride myself on covering this area. We have at least 90% original material and that makes me proud. Almost all the stuff is done in house, except the occasional results from Mississippi.

Oh...and I like Psycho and Pappy, but I get tired of looking at them also. [laughs]

**-What is up with stars for matches?**

Dave Meltzer always used stars for his matches. It was a system that was created by Jim Cornette and his friend Norm Dooley. It was given for their enjoyment of the matches and how the match was structured. It is something I have adopted and find it funny how sometimes guys ask, "How many stars was that??"

**-Why do you hate Mississippi wrestling so much?**

Mississippi is a long drive for me. I have been to very few shows, but when I go – it seems to be worse than anything I have ever seen. I have to stick by anything I have ever said about that area in the past. If they ever do anything I like, I say it. I think the stuff they are doing at EPW right now is fun. They have some talent in Rodney Mack, Gary Valiant, Sarge O'Reilly, Bitty Little and Jimmy Blaylock. I enjoy watching all those guys. The angle they are doing right now with Valiant and Blaylock is good and fun to watch.

**For Full interview go to http://rasslinriotnews.blogspot.com/2010/10/conversation-with-brian-tramel-by-brian.html**

**-Tommy Mercer talks about background and working for TNA.**

If anyone has been paying attention, it's no secret before I started wrestling that I was in the Army for 5 years with the 101st Airborne Division with 2 tours in Iraq. I've been a pro wrestling fan my whole life, but during my last tour in Iraq, I decided it was what I wanted to do. Jeff "Crippler" Daniels originally trained me. I have had the opportunity to travel with and learn a lot from Jerry Lynn, Chase Stevens, and many others.

**-We reported recently about your appearance at TNA. Tell the readers how did that work for you?? What is the TNA office saying about your future with them?**

Yeah, I spent 4 days down in Orlando with TNA. AWESOME, AWESOME, AWESOME time! Wrestled the X Division Champ Jay Lethal in a dark match. It couldn't have gone any better than it did. Got a lot of great feedback and things are looking positive. There's nothing else I want more in life so hopefully it all works out soon. Also, while on that topic, there are a lot of people on the internet who think they are a lot smarter than they really are. I've heard about the comments that the only reason that WWE and TNA even looked at me was the way I look. Nothing else. Listen, I got into this business with one goal and that's to reach the top as fast as I can, and so far I think I'm on the right track. With that being said I take pride in my appearance. I work out and do cardio because I know for a fact that you aren't taken seriously by either company if you're overweight and out of shape. (See question about advice to others for more on that.) So to whoever said I got a tryout strictly because of my look...you're almost right...and at the same time, you're almost stupid. The military instilled great discipline in me, and I think that has helped so much with the way things are moving now. I train hard still to this day on top of working 3 to 4 shows a week and traveling all over the United States. I practice promos, not on what I want to say, but practice emotion in my voice and facials while talking. I constantly watch my matches on TV to critique and fix the small things I see wrong with what I do. So all I am saying is, if you don't like me that's fine, because I know there is always a critic out there, but I work hard, and I dare you to come catch a show I'm on and tell me otherwise. Until then, don't risk carpal tunnel by typing anymore nonsense. That's the last I'll speak of that...ever.

For Full interview go to: http://rasslinriotnews.blogspot.com/2010/10/wednesday-conversation-with-tommy.html

-Terrance Ward talks about leaving ASWF and working NEW.

-First off, let's talk about your recent departure from ASWF. You have been with that company for a while and seemed to end with a dispute.

I started my wrestling career with the ASWF at the age of 16 in December of 2006 and ended it on October 9, 2010. Now, as to the details of why I quit, I am going to keep it between me and the promoter David Walls and those who were there that night. I feel it would be more professional to leave the dispute in the locker room. I do not hold any grudges against David Walls and wish him the best in the future including the ASWF Crew.

-You have become the main face of NEW when it comes to announcing, doing a lot of shows solo. What kind of pressure is that?

Well, I don't like to be considered the main face of NEW. I feel that my partner John Steele deserves a lot of credit for the work he does and has done for NEW. When it comes to announcing shows solo, for one it's a lot of pressure because for most of the show your voice is the only one that is heard. You are constantly doing numerous jobs, announcing, time keeping, and introductions, with that the pressure is intense. Not to mention it's NEW, the only Mid-South Promotion to be on TV for two consecutive years. [Taping TV for over 100 weeks - on TV since 2.10] So that on its own is a lot of pressure. It's unlike house shows where the announcing is over the PA, this is taped for TV. So not only is the live audience listening to you; the TV audience is as well.

http://rasslinriotnews.blogspot.com/2010/11/wednesday-conversation-with-terrance.html

-Dustin Starr joined RRO after his release from the WWE. Full interview posted below.

-First off, welcome back from FCW and back to the Memphis area. Let the readers of RRO first know - what happened with the release??

It's great to be back home. I mean that from the bottom of my heart. I've missed all of my friends and family so very much. In the ten months I've been gone, I feel like I've missed so much. So, it's certainly good to be back.

As far as what happened with the release? Well, nothing happened. Nothing in particular lead to my release. It's just something that happens in this business, and we have to learn to live with it. I'm not bitter. I'm not mad. I'm confident that I'll be back, one day, in a different capacity than what I was in this time around.

The release is the nature of the beast. I was told that my "passion was with performing and entertaining & not necessarily refereeing." I couldn't agree more. I'm a performer. That's what I do. So, no hard feelings. I left on very good terms.

**-Did working as a ref bother you as much as it seems to bother people in this area?? I heard many times about how you were "just a ref," even though you were working for the #1 wrestling company in the world.**

I have a feeling that it bothered others a LOT more than it bothered me. When I changed my Twitter account to "Daniel Skyler" and updated the photo, I was blown up with responses. It was a shock to so many people. The wrestlers in the area were thinking, "if he can't make it as a wrestler there, then how am I going to make it there as a wrestler?" I've heard it so many times. And my fans, well, they were just disappointed.

I had a job. A great job. I was in the ring with some of the best athletes in the world of wrestling. I trained with the likes of Ricky Steamboat, Dusty Rhodes, Dr. Tom Prichard, Norman Smiley, Road Warrior Animal, Jamie Noble, Dean Malenko, Mideon, Mike Graham, Jim Ross...the list is endless.

"Just a ref" is the dumbest thing I've ever heard. Of course, I wanted to wrestle. But when you're given an opportunity, you take it.

**-You were there when the Nexus group made their debut. Was it something that FCW planned for them or where you in on any of that?**

No. FCW had nothing to do with any of it. The group was just about to start NXT when I arrived. All of them were very nice and very professional. It was no surprise that they're becoming stars.

The angle was so strong, in fact, that the Nexus guys weren't being used on FCW TV or on the FCW Live Events. They were just so powerful.

**-Any guys that in your opinion, people should be looking for "coming up" from FCW??**

Oh yeah.  Certainly.  There are guys that I loved working with there.  Whether it was reffing or wrestling, it was always a pleasure to be in the ring with, because they knew what they were doing.

Richie Steamboat and I became very good friends.  He'll be there.  Seth Rollins (former Tyler Black) will be there.  Big E Langston was one of my favorites there.  Trent Barretta, mark my words, will be the next HBK.  He's unbelievable, in the ring.  Xavier Woods & Wes Brisco...the list goes on and on.  The crop of NXT guys, right now in Season 4, are very, very good.  I recommend everyone watching.

There are so many talented guys on the roster.  You'll be seeing more and more of them, as time passes.  WWE needs them.

**-Is the door open at the WWE??  Do you expect to go back?**

Of course, the door is open at WWE.  I will continue to work shows with them, as I always have.  And as far as being signed again, I think it's definitely a possibility.  I was told to go out and work.  Keep them up to date on what I'm doing and where I'm doing it.  So, that's what I'll do.

A friend of mine told me a few days ago, "you keep going.  You never give up on dreams, no matter what.  Chase them for the rest of your life." She's right.  And that's what I'm going to do.

**-Would you consider working TNA now??**

Absolutely.

**-I think this is important to the many workers that read this - what is some simple advice you could give to them about getting a job??**

Get in the gym.  Get in the ring.  Work hard.  Work a lot.  WATCH WRESTLING.  And send tapes.

There's a stigma among the indies that you shouldn't watch WWE.  You shouldn't watch TNA.  Why not?  If that's where you want to be, you better watch.

**-What are your plans right now?  RRO has heard rumors of you going to NEW?**

I will be in NEW on December 10th.  I will not be wrestling.  I will be doing an interview there.  I've also come to an agreement with the Mississippi RiverKings' hockey team to be their emcee at all home games, once again.  I'm keeping busy.

I probably will not wrestle until January. I need to get my body back in shape and workout in the ring a bit, to get the rust off. I will be ready when the time comes. Don't worry.

I want to thank all of my friends and fans for all of the support. I'd like to thank WWE and FCW for allowing me to live my dream. Dr. Tom Prichard, Steve Keirn and Norman Smiley are true professionals and I will never forget how much they've helped me. Also, Alfred "Simpson", I owe you a big thank you, as well. I appreciate all the hard work on the shows that I was able to perform on.

Follow me on Twitter at http://twitter.com/dustinstarr

Friend me on Facebook at

http://www.facebook.com/profile.php?id=100000784579931%23!/pages/Dustin-Starr/162743233764401

## 2010 AWARDS

-"First 120 Days of 2010" by Brian Tramel 5.20.10

----Wrestler – This really has to be the hardest year to pick so far. I can only think of a few guys that "stand out". This award is not always the best worker, but mainly goes to the guy that is making the biggest impact. Matt Riviera is that man this year. His work with TCW and RCW has made him one of the guys I like to watch this year. I think he is THE stand out. Austin Lane might be a second place vote for the ASWF/RCW switcheroo, and having his name on the lips of everyone. I would pick a guy like Christian Jacobs or Jon Michael Worthington in third just for the "potential" of what they are going to do this year.

----MVP Performer – This has nothing to do with impact or drawing power – just what worker performs the best night after night. I have a long list of guys here and that is a good thing. This category is cluttered this year and it makes me proud that guys are trying to learn their craft. Of Pokerface, Christian Jacobs, Derrick King, Eric Wayne, Austin Lane, Greg Anthony, Stan Lee, Jon Michael Worthington, Seth Knight and Alan Steele, I will have to go with Pokerface, Alan Steele, and Eric Wayne as my favorites to watch this year with all the others VERY close behind.

----Tag Team – "Midnight Gold" [Greg Anthony/Bobby Eaton] have probably been featured in more angles, matches and such this year than last year. Since they seem to be a favorite, then I would put them as one of the top three. "Asylum" [Psycho/Pappy] should always be mentioned here and really deserve to win it once. "LSD" [Cody Only/Idol Bane/Deadly Dale] are probably my favorite team to watch right now. They are just totally different than anything else in the area. "Premiere Brutality" [Kid Nikels/Eric Wayne] should also be considered in the top class here.

----MVP Tag Team – Hardest working team?? "Gold" won this award last year primarily due to the fact that they were considered a "mvp" team in the sense of helping draw a crowd. I would give this to the three teams that are the hardest working. Four teams come to mind – "Devils Reject/East Coast Bad Boys", Kid/Wayne, "High Stakes" [Chris O'Neal/Stan Lee] [if they tag all year they will be hard to beat], and Dell Tucker/Rockin Randy.

----Promotion – Another hard one to pick this year. Hub City Wrestling [aka Memphis Wrestling stars on some shows] and CWA have had the best crowds. RCW and NEW are my two favorite promotions and would get a nod. NBW is also fun and draws good crowds at big shows. I would go with RCW, NBW and NEW if I had to pick three promotions.

----Other awards….

*Most Improved: Justin Smart, Jeremy Moore and Pappy
*Most Underrated: Chris Rocker [probably the most underrated worker in the area that has good matches week after week. Also in the "Alan Steele" mode of not winning an award yet from RRO.]
*Rookie: Dan Matthews, Kevin Charles, and Blaine Devine [even though he got a nomination last

year, he probably fits more here]. Dan Matthews – hands down!!

*Best Booker: Crowds, it would have to be Rodney Grimes. Creativity – Brian Thompson.

*Best Announcer: Brian Thompson, John Steele, and Terrance Ward

*Best Manager: Rashard Devon, Athena Eclipse, and Hollywood Jimmy

*Arena Report Match of the Year: Derrick King vs Christian Jacobs 2.27.10 Ripley, TN [****], Stan Lee vs Greg Anthony Trumann, AR 4.02.10 [***3/4], Tasha Simone/"Asylum" [Psycho/Pappy] vs Worm/Suicide/Adrian Banks 3.20.10 [***3/4] and Austin Lane vs Mike Antony 4.03.10 Tuckerman, AR

*TV Match of the Year: Seth Knight vs Christian Jacobs [RCW], Seth Knight vs Justin Smart [RCW] and Seth Knight vs Rodney Mack [RCW]. Knight is a real good TV wrestler. Others: Kid Nikels vs Alan Steele [NEW] [Kid takes a chair] and Bishop vs Carnage Antwone [IWA].

*Best Wrestling Web Site: Wrestling News Center – Tia and D-Rock are two of my favorite wrestling peeps!!

*Columnist: Pokerface, TGB, and Eric Wayne

*Best Ref: Downtown Bruno, Chuck Poe, and Tom Simon

*Best Gimmick: "LSD", "Asylum", and Matt Riviera

*Horizon Award: Matt Riviera, Christian Jacobs, Pokerface, Seth Knight

*Spot Moondog Brawler of the Year: Bishop, Pappy, Deadly Dale

Closing…

----It is funny that after four years, you still have guys like Austin Lane, Derrick King, Rashard Devon, Greg Anthony, Stan Lee, Hollywood Jimmy and the "Asylum" are all placing in the same categories. I think the top categories - Wrestler & Tag Team [cover shots] – are just totally wide open this year and if voted on right now – it would be a major toss up

**-Eric Wayne had a series called "Secrets of the South" that gave readers a look at wrestlers from a wrestler's point of view.**

**Secrets of the South**

When you take a look at RRO or WNC, one thing always seems apparent - too many shows with bad talent. But I think we've all read enough negative things in the last couple of weeks, so I won't gripe about bad talent anymore. Let's face it, most of us recognize bad talent when we see it…if not, then maybe YOU are the bad talent.

I've read so much about "so-n-so" working for a decade or more, but he's still horrible. We can all say that by then, you should have a job if you're talented right? Not necessarily. Look at Alan Steele, TGB, Derrick King, Jon Micheal, Stan Lee, Pokerface…the list goes on. All of these guys should have contracts or gone farther than they have. I'm not knocking them either; they're among the most respected guys in this area and have done a lot outside of here as well. But why haven't they done more?? It's hard to say since we all have our own lives outside of wrestling…I'm actually glad that they're around now because without them, I wouldn't have learned as much as I have. Enough about them though, this column is about the other secrets of the south.

A while back I wrote about Indy legends, the guys that at any minute you could see on national TV and not be surprised because they've been in the business and know what they're doing. The next couple of guys are ones that have just started in the last few years and are taking all the advice they can to improve. It's what this business desperately needs. Someone that's hungry to make it to the next level and isn't content going to the same weekend shows.

The first guy is someone that I finally had the chance to wrestle recently at NEW, and he didn't let me down. In fact, I started putting him over to TGB the next time we talked. I'm not sure how long he's been wrestling but he has a bright future ahead of him. He's one of those guys that doesn't seem to care what you need or want out of him, he'll do it the best he can as long as he's safe. There aren't very many guys like that around here. So many guys have a hard time taking constructive criticism, but he takes it all in and WANTS to be better. Jon Allen is his name and if you don't know him yet, you will. He came to NEW a couple of months ago and is now a mainstay for as long as he is available. If you see his name on the card, buy a ticket and enjoy!

Another guy that I consider a secret of the south is Shawn Reed. The first time I met him was in 2004 when we were doing TV in Columbus, MS with Robert Gibson. He wasn't around for long and there was a reason for that...he had yet to become the performer he is today, aka he sucked! I can say that now and not worry about getting any heat because Shawn knows how much I respect him and that I wouldn't say anything that wasn't true. He had potential 6 years ago and he is still capitalizing on it. He's become one of the most consistent guys in this area and a guy I consider a big secret right now. Being in the ring with Shawn is always fun because no matter what, you know it'll be an easy night. He understands the psychology of a match and is so good on the mic that you can't help but enjoy him. He's a bit bigger than Jon but you'd never notice it the way he moves, at times. Shawn considers himself a "bottom rope luchador" but is no different than anyone else...if he feels safe, he'll do whatever you want. Again, if you see his name on the card...buy a ticket!

There are a lot more people out there that have the potential to do big things. Whether or not they actually do it is up to them. In a business that can kill you one day or give you a money-making career the next, it's hard to justify the risks we take. It's hard to explain driving hundreds of miles and coming home with very little. It takes a lot of dedication, heart, pride, and time to be the best, and the ones who are truly deserving sometimes never make it. Thankfully for all of us, they don't give up. It's a never say die attitude for all of us. Without the generations before us, we wouldn't have anyone to learn from and there would be no Indy legends. There would be no secrets of the south. Without some sort of guidance, none of us are any better than the next guy. It's what you do with the critiques you're given that make up the wrestler you become. If the Indy legends and secrets of the south are any indication, business is actually picking up...you unfortunately just have to try really hard to find the bright spots.

Here we go again! **Secrets of the South, Round 2.** There are a ton of guys around this area, and every area really, that just wrestle as a hobby. They're content with impressing their friends and don't mind staying within 100 miles of their house whenever they wrestle. But then there are the other guys. In this case, I've termed them the "Secrets of the South". Real wrestlers that WANT to improve. They WANT a career. They WANT to go other places. They WANT criticism and WANT to capitalize on any opportunity they have available to them. They WANT to be professional wrestlers and nothing else. It's been my dream since I can remember, sitting upstairs at the Mid-South Coliseum telling Jerry Jarrett to be quiet so I could watch a Jeff Gaylord match. So who is in round 2??

The first guy is someone that I've only been in the ring with a handful of times. There was even a time when, for whatever reason, we had heat between us. WE never had a problem with each other (that I know of), but the heat was created. Maybe it's because we were trained at the two top schools in this area, I'm not sure. But the guy I'm talking about is Cody Melton. We were a tag team last year for one night and seemed to flow like we'd been tagging forever. When Cody first started, he made the same mistakes as all of us, but he always seemed different. You could tell he was taking in the critiscm and wanted to improve. After not being around him for a while we had the chance to wrestle each other in 3 tags at the first Memphis tapings and tore it up. The fact that he went other places and had DK to mentor him definitely helped. I remember a guy in Ripley that didn't understand psychology that well but on TV he was a different person. It's proof that to improve you HAVE to go other places and learn everything you can. Cody is one of those guys that can have an old 80's style Memphis match or a technical match or a spotfest or really anything you need. He's a plus to any show and we all need to keep an eye on him because if things keep going the way they are, he could be a big draw one day.

The next guy is a multi-time award winner. He's a well-known name in the area as well. He has also developed a bad attitude towards wrestling as of late, and it's keeping him from fulfilling his dream. I've never had a bad match against him and in fact, we've scared people at times with the style we work. He might be more well-known as the Baron Malkavain, but I call him Dustin Ring. He was a backyarder that wrestled on his high school team. What more could you ask for? An athlete that will do crazy spots! When he's on his game, he's incredible. And even when he could care less, or is blown up, he still delivers. Whether it's the Baron or Dustin he can flat out go...chain wrestling, high spots, it doesn't matter. Even as a vampire his work adds credibility to any show he is on. If/when he ever decides to make a full time return, all promoters would be smart to book him.

Of course, not every wrestler gets in this business to have a career. But the fact that they share the same dressing room with credible athletes will never stop bothering me. The Secrets of the South are guys that deserve a full time job and years ago would've had great careers in the territories. It's a sign of the times when people that want to improve take so long to actually improve because we usually have to worry more about protecting ourselves against poorly trained "wrestlers" than taking advice and wrestling people that we CAN learn more from. All the "Secrets" are on the right track because they constantly seem to improve and it's only a matter of time before that big break is around the corner! Round 3 will be out soon, stick around and read it here first!

It's about that time, **Secrets of the South 3**! I've received a lot of good feedback for the first two installments, and I appreciate all of it. I hope no one thinks I'm just kissing ass because that's the last thing I'm worried about. The SOS are an elite group of actual wrestlers that have what it takes to forge a career in a dying business.

I've had conversations recently with people that view our business in different ways entirely. From ones that live in the past to guys that know things are changing…and everything in between. It all adds up over time and while some of us are well-rounded there are others that have no clue. SOS would be the first group of people, the ones that get it.

The first guy in this installment is someone that I met when I first started almost four years ago. Back then, he was just another guy on the card. Since then he's improved a lot and deserves everything he gets. When I first met him, I'll admit, I wrote him off as just another guy that shouldn't be wrestling. I considered him a mark, but not in a good way, because let's face it…we're all marks to some extent. My only gripe now is that he doesn't broaden his horizons and travel very much. His name is Chris Stryker. At first his name was one of those that made you roll your eyes when you found out you were wrestling him. But now, it's a totally different story. He's one of those guys that will work as hard as he can and sincerely wants to improve. We haven't had the chance to get together in the ring lately, but everyone I talk to says he's improved a lot. It's not always about being THE best though. It's about willing to and trying to improve. Of course, having credible work is a must as well. I always hear about guys that "improve" and their work is still horrible. So what the hell improved? Stryker isn't that guy. His work is credible and he is still improving. Let's hope he keeps it up!

Another guy that doesn't try near as hard as he should is everyone's favorite cruiserweight…Tatt2! He's almost in the same boat as Dustin Ring except he still takes bookings. The downside is wondering if he'll be there at belltime. I recently booked him for a benefit show because he can get over with any crowd like no other. He understands psychology a hell of a lot better than people give him credit for as well. A few people came up to me after seeing him at one show and he was one of the first things they mentioned. From high flying to technical wrestling, Tatt2 is one of those guys that can bring a hell of a show anytime he steps in the ring. He's the best at making a fast paced, high flying match make sense. It's never just a bunch of high spots thrown together, and there aren't many at this level that can do that. If Tatt2 didn't feel the way he does about local wrestling, and promoters were smarter, then not only would Tatt2 be seen more often, but so would a lot of other guys.

Take note people, I'm not writing just because I'm bored. SOS are wrestlers that no one seems to book properly or if they do, they aren't booked enough. We all need to keep striving to improve, it's how often we take the lessons we learn and apply them next time we wrestle that makes the difference. All these guys as well as a dozen others actually take pride in what they do every time out and the more we ALL take pride in our appearance and work…the better business will be for all of us.

**-Coach's Corner "Road to Wrestler of the Year" by Brian Tramel  7.07.10**

----This is a road that has been traveled by only seven individuals since the start of RRO.  Those travelers were Derrick King, Dustin Starr, Rodney Mack, Kevin White, Austin Lane, Danny B Goode and Flash Flanagan.  There were only two guys to make it to the end of the road – Derrick King and Dustin Starr.  Derrick King will always be a candidate for this award, if he continues to work the area.  Austin Lane could have the edge over Derrick King this year and be the front runner of this group of seven.  He continues to have great matches and is over with crowds at ASWF and NEW.  The only thing keeping him from getting enough votes – that he is seen by only those two crowds.  But, if King does not win again, Lane is the guy to beat on in that group of guys who have traveled this road before.

----Who else this year or in the next few years might be nominated and travel that road?  Here is a list of guys that could easily "walk that walk" and see the cover of a future edition of RRO Yearbook.

-Justin Smart – He has improved a lot over the last year.  He is a solid worker that loves the sport and is trying to season himself into being a great worker.  He would have to establish himself in more than one promotion in some high profile matches to accomplish enough votes for the award.  He is part of the future of this area though.

-Pokerface – A great worker that is one of the more technical in the area and can work different styles.  He is great - from a brawl to a shooting style to high flying to wrestling.  He is a guy you would want on your roster due to his being a team player.  He would have to push himself to be in the limelight more and be seen by more people to get votes.  He is easily one of the top guys in the area.

-Cody Melton – A young guy that has been almost snubbed by the RRO awards.  He lost two awards in the 2008 awards by a total of four votes.  He could be a major player in the future of this area – trained by Kevin White and now being mentored by Derrick King.  He should have the exposure and opportunity to push himself into the front in the next few years.

-Eric Wayne – Can a guy who's major story was him kicking someone in the face last year turn his whole career around to be one of the best in this area??  The answer is YES – I am going out on a limb here a bit, but Wayne is going to win this award in the next three years.  He is a solid worker, gets exposure, and has won his share of awards.  He has the support of the RRO fans and the wrestling community.

-Kid Nikels – Even though Wayne may have won more awards, Nikels is a "standout" from the Ken Wayne School.  He is a big guy that works hard and does anything it takes to help the promotion.  He has the potential to be the first Ken Wayne student to get a WWE developmental with more seasoning.  Nikels could easily be pushed into the limelight to get enough votes.

-Jon Michael – He is flawless. It has just surprised me that he has not won more awards. He has been exposed here with RCW and in the Nashville area for SAW. I look for him to be nominated in a few new categories this year. He has to be a leading candidate to be nominated and could win by his popularity.

-Greg Anthony – He is the best talker of the area. His work is hard to beat and he has one of the best wrestling minds in the area. His size will not matter in this area in the RRO awards. He is very well known through his association with Bobby Eaton and his exposure on RCW. Anthony could easily be a nominee, but might be considered more of a tag team wrestler this year.

-Christian Jacobs – He has always been a major undercard babyface in the area. This year has seen him get his push to main event babyface status in EWE and RCW. What happens when your workrate starts matching your popularity?? It makes it easier to be nominated for the big awards, and I look for Jacobs to get a lot of interest this year.

-Tatt2 – All the talent in the world, but always seems to find it hard to put together the whole package. He has become a solid worker and seems to understand how to put together a match. Every time I have seen him perform the fans really get into his act. If the fans and workers got behind him, he might have a chance in the voting. I don't see him being in the race this year, but I think he will get some nominations in other categories.

-Bishop – He has the size. He has improved his skills and is fun to listen to on the mic. He needs more seasoning, but in time, he may get the nod for this award and win a nomination. He works in various promotions and gets himself on TV as much as possible. A more solid fan base will make him popular and help him be nominated.

-Alan Steele – He won his first award in 2009 and continues to keep his name out there this year. Steele has not been working steady the whole RRO era, but has kept a steady schedule this year. He works TCW, RCW and NEW – and is considered the top guy on all those rosters – in and out of the dressing room. He is probably more deserving of an award like this than anyone, but does he have enough people and impact this year to do it??

-Matt Riviera – As I stated in a past *Corner*, this award does not always go to the best worker, but mainly goes to the guy that is making the biggest impact. Matt Riviera is that man this year. His work with TCW and RCW has made him one of the guys I like to watch this year. Does he have enough support to help him get nominated??

-Jeremy Moore – This guy making the list will probably surprise people the most. Could he win this award this year? He has made a huge impact in the Dyersburg area and continues to improve in the ring. I can't see enough support from the wrestling community to see him nominated this year, but if he continues on the path he is taking, then he could be considered one of the top guys in the next three years.

-Seth Knight – This guy is probably the dark horse of the whole crew. He has sat back for years being a better than average worker. Exposure on RCW TV has made everyone take notice that Knight is good at whatever he is asked to do – a squash for Rodney Mack or go toe to toe with Alan Steele. His stint with RCW this year has most of the guys that have worked with him talking about how easy he is to work with and how good he can be. His fan base may help get him a nomination, but he will have to have his peers help him win.

-Albino Rhino – This guy is a monster!! If it was 1985, Jerry Lawler would be main eventing against him. Why isn't Lawler using him now?? The reason he wasn't considered is that he is working just a limited schedule now. If he ever got into the mode of working 2 to 3 shows a week, and different shows, this guy would have an impact. He needs the desire to push himself. The right person sees this guy, and he will be working big shows.

-Kevin White – I did mention him as one of the seven that have been nominated in the past four years, but would this guy have a chance to be nominated or win this year?? I think so. The Memphis Wrestling TV show helped push White into the limelight in this area. If they continue to push him on TV and the ratings go up, he will be on the radar more than ever now. He may have a better chance of being nominated this year with Lane and King than anyone else.

-Maxx Corbin –This guy has done a lot this past year to get ready to be great the rest of the year. He has not worked that much, but it looks like he is going to throw himself into working more and more dates now. This guy is an asset behind the scenes, promoting and doing video work. He is the whole package much like Dustin Starr who presented that to the WWE when getting a job. Maxx can do that as a hand for a local promotion. He has to be on top in front of fans to get their votes. His peers love working him and consider him great for the dressing room.

-Chris O'Neal – Chris is one of the most popular guys in the area. I have heard crowd reactions from him in different arenas – and it is usually the same – LOUD!! If he stays in any place long enough, he becomes insanely popular in either a tag team or just as a single. It will be hard for O'Neal to win the Wrestler of the Year award, because he is usually stuck in tags with Jon Michael or Christian Jacobs, with whom he won Tag Team of The Year 2007 and was ranked second in RRO Top 10 tag teams last year. This year he is tagging with Stan Lee, which will probably see him get nominationed in that category again.

-Stan Lee – He has been a mainstay as an award winner. He has won MVP Performer two times and placed 6th or better in the RRO Top 10 the last three years. What could he do to put himself over as the Wrestler? The top guy?? He is now doing a tag team and not sure if he will ever get that desire back to get better and get a full time job in wrestling. When this guy is focused – he is the MAN in this area. When he is not focused, he is just one of those real good workers.

-Matt Boyce – This guy is almost the total package. I say "almost" because he is not quite there yet. He is highly improved in workrate, mic skills, and his look. A great looking kid that could easily be a huge star not only in this area, but also one of those guys that you could see working for the WWE. He works regularly and is seen by a lot of fans. He is liked by his peers. If they continue to push this guy on Memphis Wrestling, I look for him to get a mention in a few of the awards and might be a future Wrestler of the Year candidate.

----So will it be Derrick King and Austin Lane walking down the road of Wrestler of the Year with a new foe?? Will the fans and wrestling community surprise the area and nominate three new faces to fight over the top RRO award?? From this list of guys, how many of them will even be considered?? In four years of voting, there were only seven different guys that traveled the road. What will it take to become nominated? As the *10 To Vote* starts in January of 2011, the answers will be revealed, but until then we can just speculate and guess on the future of RRO Wrestler of the Year award.

**-Coach's Corner "2010: 2/3 Gone – Who Are the Award Leaders?" by Brian Tramel**

----The question I get the most when I post something like this is - what about "so'n'so." I see a lot of wrestling, but I do not see EVERYONE and EVERYTHING, so it is up to the readers to post their picks and make others visible. Post your responses on the Kayfabe Message Board!! And, I would love to read your thoughts just on my picks!! I have also picked more than three in some categories - I am trying to give everyone a nod that deserves it.

----Wrestler of the Year - This really has to be the hardest year to pick so far. I can only think of a few guys that "stand out". This award is not always the best worker, but mainly goes to the guy that is making the biggest impact. I honestly can not pick one guy that has stood out during the whole time. I put over Matt Riveria for this award at the 1/3 mark, but even though he continues to help promote some good shows, he is not seen as much without RCW TV. Derrick King may be the front runner now with him working so many dates and just being newsworthy in local promotions. Austin Lane would also be considered with him being in the news and continuing to have good matches. He also branched out a bit this year. I would consider maybe Greg Anthony, Jon Michael Worthington and Christian Jacobs also for their EWE/RCW work.

----MVP Performer - This has nothing to do with impact or drawing power – just what worker performs the best night after night. I have a long list of guys here and that is a good thing. Nothing has much changed in this category. There are a lot of guys that are just performing at high levels. Pokerface, Christian Jacobs, Derrick King, Eric Wayne, Austin Lane, Greg Anthony, Stan Lee, Jon Michael Worthington, Seth Knight and Alan Steele I will have to go with Pokerface, Alan Steele and Eric Wayne as my favorites to watch this year with all the others VERY close behind.

----Tag Team – "Asylum" [Psycho/Pappy] should always be mentioned here and really deserve to win it. They are probably the only true tag team left in the area. "Premiere Brutality" [Kid Nikels/Eric Wayne] are my second pick here making an impact on Memphis Wrestling and everywhere they tag, but really don't tag as much as Psycho/Pappy. "Too Cruel" [Brian Christopher/Wolfie D] are one of my favorites, but probably by the end of the year will not even be considered. "Midnight Gold" [Greg Anthony/Bobby Eaton] have probably been featured in more angles, matches and such this year than last year, but the team is pretty much done. Is it the RRO Tag Team Curse?? "LSD" [Cody Only/Idol Bane/Deadly Dale] should also be considered.

----MVP Tag Team – Hardest working team?? "Gold" won this award last year primarily due to the fact that they were considered a "mvp" team in the sense of helping draw a crowd. Only two teams come to mind – "Devils Reject/East Coast Bad Boys" and Kid Nikels/Eric Wayne. Neither team tag enough on a regular basis, so it is a hard pick. "Asylum" #3 here, because they do just basic solid psychology.

----Promotion – Hub City Wrestling [aka Memphis Wrestling stars on some shows] and CWA had the best crowds early this year. RCW and NEW are fun to watch, but one is dead now and one still doesn't draw. NBW has been drawing decent crowds all year long. ASWF draws the biggest overall weekly average, so I would put them first followed by probably NBW with Traditional Championship Wrestling/Showtime All-Star Wrestling as a nod for third. It will be hard for either of those two to win, because they are a little "outside" of our comfort zone.

OTHER AWARDS

*Most Improved:  Cody Melton, Justin Smart, Maxx Corbin, Mike Anthony, Matt Boyce, Drew Haskins, Jeremy Moore and Chris Styker
*Most Underrated:  Chris Rocker [probably the most underrated worker in the area that has good matches week after week. Also in the "Alan Steele" mode of not winning an award yet from RRO.], Seth Knight, C-Money, Kevin White, Maxx Corbin, Mark Devonci [aka OZ] and Tatt2.
*Rookie: Dan Matthews, Kevin Charles, Blaine Devine [even though he got a nomination last year, he probably fits more here] and Moe Stegall. Matthews should win, but Moe is really entertaining.
*Best Booker:  Crowds it would have to be ASWF. Creativity – Brian Thompson or the SAW crew.
*Best Announcer:  Brian Thompson, Brandon Baxter and Terrance Ward
*Best Manager:  Rashard Devon, Frank Martin and Hollywood Jimmy
*Arena Report Match of the Year:  Derrick King vs Christian Jacobs 2.27.10 Ripley, TN [****], Stan Lee vs Greg Anthony Trumann, AR 4.02.10 [***3/4], Tasha Simone/"Asylum" [Psycho/Pappy] vs Worm/Suicide/Adrian Banks Paragould, AR 3.20.10 [***3/4], Austin Lane vs Mike Antony 4.03.10 Tuckerman, AR [***3/4] and Austin Lane vs Eric Wayne West Memphis, AR 8.14.10
*TV Match of the Year:  Seth Knight vs Christian Jacobs [RCW], Seth Knight vs Justin Smart [RCW] and Seth Knight vs Rodney Mack [RCW]. Knight is a real good TV wrestler. Others:  Kid Nikels vs Alan Steele [NEW] [Kid takes a chair], Bishop vs Carnage Antwone [IWA] and Tommy Mercer vs Stan Lee [JLMW].
*Best Wrestling Web Site:  Wrestling News Center – Tia and D-Rock are two of my favorite wrestling peeps!!
*Columnist:  Pokerface, TGB and Eric Wayne
*Best Ref:  Downtown Bruno, Chuck Poe and Kaleb
*Best Gimmick:  Ike Tucker, "LSD", "Asylum", "Too Cruel" and Matt Riviera
*Horizon Award:  Matt Riviera, Tommy Mercer, Christian Jacobs, Pokerface, Seth Knight
*Spot Moondog Brawler of the Year:  Bishop, Pappy, Adrian Banks

**-Brian Tramel takes a final look at the upcoming awards before nominations in all categories.**

----Promotion of the Year 2010: If you go by just attendance on a weekly basis, you would have to pick ASWF and TIWF, who draw, on average, more than any other promotions. EPW has been entertaining. I have been told even IWA is drawing good crowds. Talent wise - NEW, EWE and defunct RCW had the best talent roster. NBW has weathered the storm and continues to draw average. My nominees: ASWF, NBW and EWE.

----Booker of the Year 2010: Who gave you the best storylines?? It is not always the best crowds here, because crowds are bad everywhere. What seem to be the most interesting?? I really enjoyed EWE, NBW, NEW and EPW stuff this year. Even though each promotion went in totally different directions, it was entertaining to read about them. NEW had to improve on the basics of their promotion and presented some good solid storylines. EPW was totally old school with some shock type storylines that I like. EWE, who did not draw great numbers, had some good stuff with the return of TGB and the whole push of Christian Jacobs. My nominees: EWE, NEW and EPW.

----Announcer of the Year 2010: Who is the best on the mic for TV or just announcing at the shows?? Brian Thompson, who worked with RCW and NEW [for one show], should be considered even though limited work. Brandon Baxter was my favorite this year, even though he was only in there for 15 weeks. Last year's winner Terrance Ward is good and along with John Steele worked the whole year. I actually look for Ward to win the award this year again. My nominees: Brian Thompson, Brandon Baxter and Terrance Ward.

----Gimmick of the Year 2010: Who has the best gimmick?? This award is wide open this year with the "vampire" being absent this year. "Asylum" [Psycho/Pappy] is probably better at their gimmick than anyone in the area. Ike Tucker, when he is a babyface, is a great gimmick. Matt Riviera lives his gimmick. "LSD" are always fun. I really liked "Too Cruel" - gimmick of two old pros forming a team. My nominees: Asylum, Matt Riviera and "Too Cruel."

----Manager of the Year 2010: "Hollywood" Jimmy Blaylock and Rashard Devon, who have fought over this award for all the past four years, will be nominated. I really like Frank Martin as a manager and he should be considered. I have heard good things about Kellen James also. My nominees: Jimmy Blaylock, Rashard Devon and Frank Martin.

----Referee of the Year 2010: Two time winner Downtown Bruno has to lead the pack here. If you have not seen him work at NEW, then you need to go for a visit. He is not your typical "out of sight out of mind" referee that I usually like, but when it comes to the time in the match where he is needed only for the 3-count, he is there. Chuck Poe comes off as a total professional – in and out of the ring. He is my top pick this year due to Bruno winning two years in a row. Caleb Demps, who worked RCW and works regular for EWE, is a real good referee also. Everyone puts over Joey Lynn also, but I have never seen him work. My nominees: Chuck Poe, Downtown Bruno and Caleb Demps.

----Wrestler: This really has to be the hardest year to pick, since the start of the site. I can only think of a few guys that "stand out". This award is not always the best worker, but mainly goes to the guy that is making the biggest impact. I honestly cannot pick one guy that has stood out during the whole time. I put over Matt Riveria for this award at the 1/3 mark, but he has not seen as much without RCW TV. Derrick King works so many dates and just being newsworthy in local promotions. Austin Lane would also be considered with him being in the news and continuing to have good matches. He also branched out a bit this year. Lane is also the guy that has won almost every major award here at RRO, but has never won the BIG one. **My top pick would be Lane and it should be the year that he wins.** I would consider Greg Anthony, Jon Michael Worthington [health problems and battled back to wrestle and book EWE] and Christian Jacobs also for their EWE/RCW work. My nominees: Austin Lane, Derrick King and Jon Michael.

----MVP Performer: This has nothing to do with impact or drawing power – just what worker performs the best night after night. I have a long list of guys here and that is a good thing. Nothing has much changed in this category. There are a lot of guys that are just performing at high levels. Pokerface, Christian Jacobs, Derrick King, Eric Wayne, Austin Lane, Greg Anthony, Stan Lee, Jon Michael Worthington, Seth Knight and Alan Steele. My nominees: Greg Anthony, Christian Jacobs and Pokerface.

----Tag Team: "Asylum" [Psycho/Pappy] should always be mentioned here and really deserve to win it. **I honestly believe it is their year**, because of their continuing to work major promotions and being over. They are probably the only true tag team left in the area. "Premiere Brutality" [Kid Nikels/Eric Wayne] made an impact on Memphis Wrestling and everywhere they tag, but really don't tag as much as Psycho/Pappy. "Derrick King Enterprises" [Derrick King/Drew Haskins/Sista O'Feelyah] work mainly in Nashville, but should be considering - being a regular top tag team all the year. "Too Cruel" [Brian Christopher/Wolfie D] were one of my favorites, but did not see much action. "Midnight Gold" [Greg Anthony/Bobby Eaton] have probably been featured in more angles, matches and such this year than last year, but the team is pretty much done. "LSD" [Cody Only/Idol Bane/Deadly Dale] should also be considered. My nominees: "Asylum", "Derrick King Enterprises" and "Too Cruel".

----MVP Tag Team: Hardest working team?? Only two teams come to mind – "Devils Reject/East Coast Bad Boys" and Kid Nikels/Eric Wayne. Nikels/Wayne get my main nod here, because they have worked more as a team and are hard working. "Picture Perfect" actually worked more in Nashville area as a team, but should be considered here. The team of Chris O'Neal and Stan Lee also were good, but did not tag that much. "Gold" also because they did headline some big shows. My nominees: Nikels/Wayne, ECBB/DR and "Picture Perfect".

----Rookie of The Year: This award goes to someone that worked at least 26 dates in their first year of wrestling. The top ones that come to mind are Dan Matthews, Kevin Charles, Moe Stegall and Blaine Devine. Devine was on the ballot last year, but got stuck between both years and might get a nod. My nominees: Dan Matthews, Moe Stegall and Blaine Devine.

----Spot Moondog Brawler of the Year Award: This will be our second year to present this award and I would like to see someone new win it, even though Psycho still does more hardcore than anyone. This award has been given a stamp of approval by the family of Spot Moondog. My first two picks are also guys that have been hardcore in this area for years and deserve the nod. My nominees: Motley Cruz, Ron Rage and Adrian Stratton [two of the craziest hardcore bouts I witnessed this year was with him].

----Horizon Award: This is the award for the guy/girl/team that you think should have a TNA/WWE contract. This award was won by Austin Lane last year. Eric Wayne amd Byron Willcott [who had a contract] in close second the year before and Dustin Starr won it in 2006 and 2007. My nominees: Christian Jacobs, Kid Nikels and Matt Riveria .

----Most Improved: Who got better in 2010? Cody Melton, Justin Smart, Maxx Corbin, Mike Anthony, Matt Boyce, Drew Haskins, Jeremy Moore and Chris Styker are all good picks. My nominees: Cody Melton, Justin Smart and Mike Anthony.

----Most Underrated: Chris Rocker [probably the most underrated worker in the area that has good matches week after week. Also in the "Alan Steele" mode of not winning an award yet from RRO.], Seth Knight, C-Money, Kevin White, Maxx Corbin, Mark Devonci [aka OZ] and Tatt2 are all good picks. My nominees: Big Red, Chris Rocker and Chris O'Neal.

----Arena Report Match of the Year: These are the best matches that I witnessed at live events. This is hard to vote for some people because they do not see as much stuff as I do. But…if you attended one of these matches, then you know the quality of it. I have listed all the matches that scored [***3/4] or higher. Please pick three. I have **highlighted** my three picks. **Derrick King vs Christian Jacobs 2.27.10 Ripley, TN [****]**, Stan Lee vs Greg Anthony Trumann, AR 4.02.10 [***3/4], **Tasha Simone/"Asylum" [Psycho/Pappy] vs Worm/Suicide/Adrian Banks Paragould, AR 3.20.10 [***3/4]**, Austin Lane vs Mike Antony 4.03.10 Tuckerman, AR [***3/4], Stan Lee vs. Chris O'Neal vs. Seth Knight 7.03.10 Jonesboro, AR [***3/4], Austin Lane vs Eric Wayne 7.02.10 West Memphis, AR [***3/4], Eric Wayne vs Kid Nikels 8.14.10 West Memphis, AR [***3/4], First Blood Elimination: Kid Nikels/Eric Wayne vs Justin Smart/Shawn Reed 10.08.10 West Memphis, AR [****] and **Derrick King vs Stan Lee 12.17.10 Blytheville, AR [****]**.

----TV Match of the Year: These are original matches that aired on TV this year. I have **highlighted** by three picks. If you think I missed one, then feel free to nominate it. **Derrick King, Christian Jacobs & Cody Melton vs. Bobby Eaton, "Golden Boy" Greg Anthony & Jon Michael Worthington [RCW]** - real fun bout with a tremendous angle with Alan Steele at the end - favorite TV bout of the year!! **Seth Knight vs Christian Jacobs [RCW]**, Seth Knight vs Justin Smart [RCW] and Seth Knight vs Rodney Mack [RCW]. Knight is a real good TV wrestler. Others: Kid Nikels vs Alan Steele [NEW] [Kid takes a chair], **Bishop vs Carnage Antwone [IWA]** and Tommy Mercer vs Stan Lee [JLMW].

----Best Wrestling Web Site: What other sites besides this site?? www.wrestlingnewscenter.com, The Mid-Southern Message Board and www.georgiawrestlinghistory.com are my nominees.

----Columnist of the Year: Who has the best columns?? I have to mention Loose Cannon, Randall Lewis, and Eric Wayne. My nominees this year are Greg Anthony, Downtown Bruno and Pokerface.

----Female Performer: Not that many girls left working on regular basis - week after week. The Ga-Ga Girl had Memphis Wrestling exposure, but was bad. My nominees: Tasha Simone [my favorite this year, because of winning the NWA Title and participating in a MOTY candidate], Athena Eclipse and Su Yung.

# 2010
# AWARD WINNERS!!

## Site of the Year
# Wrestling News Center
Mid Southern Message Board [-70]
GeorgiaWrestlingHistory.com [-95]

2009: Wrestling News Center
2008: Wrestling News Center
2007: Mid-Southern Message Board
2006: www.hollywoodjimmy.com/DustinStarr.com [tie]

----The last three years this site has been established as THE site.  It was not even a race with them winning by 70% over second place.

FOUR FUN FACTS

-Site is owned and operated by Tia and Jimmy Blaylock.
-Site's infamous message board was changed this year.
-The site is Mississippi based with emphasis on local promotions in that area.
-The site features a collection of stories from all over the world.

**Columnist of the Year**
# Greg Anthony
Eric Wayne [-52]
Downtown Bruno [-54]

2009: Greg Anthony
2008: Brian Thompson
2007: Gene Jackson
2006: Loose Cannon


----Anthony led the race the whole time leading with about the same amount during the whole time.  He has become a favorite of the site and his column is featured on various other sites.

FIVE FUN FACTS

-The Golden Circle, his column, became a feature in 2009.
-He was managed by Coach BT [Brian Tramel] in a feud with Bobby Eaton, who was managed by Brian Thompson, earlier in his career.
-He is a father of two sons.
-He has been featured on the cover of two Yearbooks.

**Most Improved of the Year**
# Cody Melton
Justin Smart [-20]
Chris Stryker [-20]

2009: Bishop
2008: Idol Bane
2007: Rockin Randy

----Melton led the race by 20%+ during the whole time.  He has proven to be one of the best in the area by fans and his peers.

FOUR FUN FACTS

-Trained by Kevin White.
-First award he has won.
-Lost two awards in 2008 by 2 points each.
-Trained in Martial arts.

**Most Underrated of the Year**
# Seth Knight
Maxx Corbin [-12]
Chris Rocker [-18]

----Knight led the voting by 14% with a third of the voting over.  He then led by 19% at the 2/3 point.  He won the award by 12%.

2009: Alan Steele
2008: AJ Bradley
2007: Kilo

FOUR FUN FACTS

-This was his first award to win.
-He has a Transformers tattoo along with others.
-Greg Anthony is his brother-in-law.
-He used to wrestle as "Predator."

WrestlingNewsCenter.com        Taken by: Tia Blaylock

**Female Performer of the Year**
# Su Yung
Tasha Simone [-1]
Athena Eclipse [-9]

2009: Jazz
2008: Su Yung

----Su Yung fought back and forth with Tasha Simone for most of this race. She had a 11% lead at the 1/3 point, but fighting for the win the rest of the race.

FOUR FUN FACTS

-Trained by Kevin White
-Featured prominently on Jerry Lawler's Memphis Wrestling.
-Signed with WWE developmental in Florida as "Sonia."
- Dated Jerry Lawler.

**Referee of the Year**
# Caleb Demps
Downtown Bruno [-8]
Chuck Poe [-17]

2009: Downtown Bruno
2008: Downtown Bruno
2007: Bill Rush
2006: Bill Rush

----Caleb had some strong competition with Bruno this year.  It seemed like he was the leader most of the way, but Bruno kept closing in on him.  Demps held on and beat two-time winner Downtown Bruno.

FOUR FUN FACTS

-First time to be nominated for RRO award.
-Worked both RCW and EWE this year.
-One of only three guys to ever win this award.
-His mom is always at the matches along with his sister taking photos.

**Gimmick of The Year**
## "Asylum" [Psycho/Pappy]
Byron Wilcott [-30]
Precious [-40]

2009: "The Baron" Malkavain
2008: "The Baron" Malkavain
2007: The Posse
2006: The Posse

----This team has one of the only true gimmicks in the area and won this award big time. They beat the other candidates by 30% or more.

FOUR FUN FACTS

-Both have wrestled in hardcore matches.
-Featured on Memphis TV for IWA.
-Psycho carries with him his baby doll – Kayte. Kayte is the real name of Brian Tramel's oldest daughter.
-This gimmick has been nominated 2 other times.

**TV Match of the Year**
# Derrick King, Christian Jacobs & Cody Melton vs. Bobby Eaton, "Golden Boy" Greg Anthony & Jon Michael Worthington [RCW]
Tommy Mercer vs Stan Lee [JLMW] [-49]
Christian Jacobs vs Seth Knight [RCW] [-56]

2009: Dustin Starr vs. Kevin White
2008:Koko Ware/Eugene vs. Kid Kash/Kevin White with Garry White/Su Yung
2007:Johnny Dotson vs. Derrick King 9.08.07

----A 6-man tag with some of the best talent in the area.  Never had competition from other two matches beating both of them by over 45%.

FOUR FUN FACTS
-Match was from "4th in the Forest."
-First time that a 6-man tag has won this award.
-It featured the team "Picture Perfect" on opposite sides.
-Everyone that participated has won a RRO Award.

**Arena Report Match of The Year**

# Austin Lane vs. Eric Wayne 7.02.10 West Memphis, AR [***3/4]

Derrick King vs Stan Lee 12.17.10 Blytheville, AR [****] [-3]
Tasha Simone/"Asylum" [Psycho/Pappy] vs Worm/Suicide/Adrian Banks
Paragould, AR 3.20.10 [***3/4] [-15]

2009: Austin Lane vs Eric Wayne West Memphis, AR 10.09.09 [****]
2008: Kid Nikels vs. Eric Wayne [****1/4] West Memphis, AR 2.10.08
2007: Ripley Street Fight: "Hot Topic" [Stan Lee/Derrick King] vs. "The Posse" [Simon Reed/Lil Chris] Ripley, TN 8.11.07 [[****1/4]

----The battle was with the top two matches going back and forth.
Lane/Wayne pulled it out at the end.

FOUR FUN FACTS

-Wayne has won this award three years in a row.
-Austin Lane has been nominated for this award with 4 different matches.
-First time two participants won this award two years in a row.
-The same building has housed MOTY for three years straight.

**Jimmy Blaylock & Brandon Baxter**

**Announcer of the Year**
# Brandon Baxter
Terrance Ward [-8]
Brian Thompson [-15]

----Terrance Ward and Brandon Baxter fought for this one, but Baxter seems to be the popular pick.  This was Baxter's rookie year as an announcer.

2009: Terrance Ward
2008: Brian Thompson
2007: Michael Ward
2006: Michael Thomas

FOUR FUN FACTS
-Full time job as a DJ for Kiss-FM in Jonesboro, AR.
-He began his career at a young age on Global Wrestling.
-He was nominated for MOTY in 2007.
-He was a regular and helped with booking for Power Pro Wrestling.

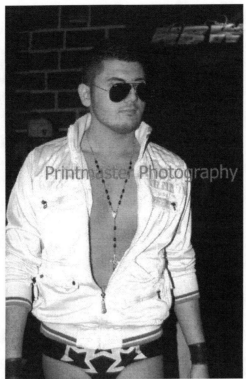

**Photo by Rick Nelson [Printmaster photograph]**

**Booker of the Year**
# Jeremy Moore – NBW
Jon Michael – EWE [-15]
NEW Committee [-22]

2009: NEW Committee
2008: Greg Anthony
2007: TLCW Committee
2006: TLCW Committee

----Many viewed him as just a kid before entering the year, but he ended it being the only surviving Dyersburg area promotion.  He led the race most of the way and took it by 15%.

FOUR FUN FACTS

-He loves the TV show "Jersey Shore."
-He bought the other Dyersburg based promotion MACW early this year.
-His step dad – Jeff McDonald – helps him run the promotion.
-He was trained by Sir MO.

## Promotion of the Year
## ASWF
NEW [-4]
EWE [-9]

2009: NEW
2008: ASWF
2007: TLCW
2006: TLCW

----This was a three way fight with two promotions that have excellent talent [NEW/EWE] and a promotion that outdraws both of them.  ASWF took this award in the final days winning it for their second time.

FOUR FUN FACTS
-David Walls and Ricky Rowland are the current owners.
-Week after week draw more fans than any other promotion.
-Brian Christopher worked most of the year here.
-Austin Lane finished the year as their champion.

**Horizon Award**
# Kid Nikels
Alan Steele [-11]
Matt Riviera [-21]

2009: Austin Lane
2008: Eric Wayne
2007: Dustin Starr
2006: Dustin Starr

----Nikels and Steele fought it out with Riviera being a distant third. Kid took over and took the win.

FOUR FUN FACTS
-He is a fan of serial killers and references them in his interviews.
-He attended a WWE camp in Louisville and they were impressed with him.
-He was trained by Ken Wayne and won MOTY in 2008.
-Regular tag team partner with Eric Wayne as "Premiere Brutality."

## Manager of the Year
# "Hollywood" Jimmy Blaylock
Kellen James [-19]
Frank Martin [-49]

2009: Brian Thompson
2008: "Hollywood" Jimmy Blaylock
2007: "Hollywood" Jimmy Blaylock
2006: Rashard Devon

----Blaylock won this award two years in a row and then lost last year, but returns as three time Manager of the Year by 19% over second place Kellen James. Frank Martin finished way out of the race 49% behind Blaylock.

FOUR FUN FACTS
-He has been featured on the Conan O'Brien TV show.
-Jerry Lawler has been known to buy crowns from Blaylock's costume store.
-He was featured on Jerry Lawler's Memphis Wrestling.
-He was featured in a big angle with Gary Valiant in EPW.

**Moondog Spot Brawler of the Year**
# Motley Cruz
Psycho [-7]
Pappy [-37]

2009: Psycho

----Cruz took the lead in this race at the start and stuck in there until the end. Last year's winner Psycho finished 7% behind him.

FOUR FUN FACTS

-He lost this award last year by one vote.
-He wrestled the majority of the year in NBW and TIWF.
-He can been seen on youtube wrestling Ric Flair -
http://www.youtube.com/watch?v=idFZO13H5Zo
-This is Cruz's first award.

## Rookie of the Year
# Dan Matthews
Kevin Charles [-4]
Moe Stegall [-7]

2009: JD Kerry
2008: Greg King Jr
2007: Ramsey Cahill
2006: Lil Chris

----Matthews beats the other two Ken Wayne trainees to win the award. It was back and forth with him and Charles. Stegall was in third during the whole race. Matthews wins it by 4%.

FOUR FUN FACTS

-Trained by Ken Wayne.
-He formed a team called "Prime Danger" with Kevin Charles.
-He won the US Jr Title this year beating Austin Lane.
-He is an IT tech and helps backstage at NEW TV.

**MVP Tag Team of the Year**
## "Asylum" [Psycho/Pappy]
"Premiere Brutality" [Eric Wayne/Kid Nikels] [-6]
 "Picture Perfect" [Christian Jacobs/Jon Michael] [-11]

2009: "Midnight Gold" [Greg Anthony/Bobby Eaton] with Brian Thompson
2008: "Hot Topic" [Derrick King/Stan Lee]
2007: "Naughty By Nature" [Rude/Pokerface]
2006: "Family of Pain" [Mickey Ray/Sarge O'Reilly]

----This was a two team race with "Picture Perfect" a distant third. "Premiere Brutality" led a bit of the way, but "Asylum" took it in the final day.

FOUR FUN FACTS

-They won the NWA Southern Tag Team Titles this year.
-This is the third incarnation of the team to be nominated.
-Donald and David are their real names.
-First time nominated for this award.

**MVP Performer**
# Greg Anthony
Alan Steele [-13]
Stan Lee [-16]

2009: Austin Lane
2008: Stan Lee
2007: Stan Lee
2006: Austin Lane

----Lee and Steele didn't finish far behind Anthony, but Anthony led the whole race. Lee and Austin Lane were the only two guys that had won this award until now.

FOUR FUN FACTS

-One of only three guys who have won this award.
-He won Tag Team of the Year and MVP Team last year.
-He becomes the first person to win both Wrestler and MVP in one year.
-He has a movie collection of over 600 titles.

WrestlingNewsCenter.com
Taken by: Tia Blaylock

**Tag Team of the Year**
# "Asylum" [Psycho/Pappy]
"Picture Perfect" [Christian Jacobs/Jon Michael/Chris O'Neal] [-6]
"LSD" [Idol Bane/Deadly Dale/Cody Only] [-26]

2009: "Midnight Gold" [Greg Anthony/Bobby Eaton] with Brian Thompson
2008: "Black Label Society" [AJ Bradley/Robbie Douglas/Void]
2007: "The Posse" [Simon Reed/Lil Chris]
2006: "Picture Perfect" [Christian Jacobs/Jon Michael/Chris O'Neal]

----This was a battle back and forth with the two top teams. "Asylum" took the lead and beat out "Picture Perfect" by only 6%. "LSD" came in a distant third getting beat by 26%.

FOUR FUN FACTS

-They became the second team to ever win both Tag Team and MVP Team.
-Pappy carries Trigger [a toy horse head with chain] to the ring.
-Pappy used to wrestle doing a hillbilly gimmick.
-Both guys were nominated for Spot Moondog Brawler of the Year

**Wrestler of the Year**
# Greg Anthony
Austin Lane [-1]
Derrick King [-15]

2009: Dustin Starr
2008: Derrick King
2007: Derrick King
2006: Derrick King

----This was a battle back and forth with Lane and Anthony. Anthony actually won the award by less than 1%. He scored 39.76% of the vote and Lane with 39.36% of the vote.

FOUR FUN FACTS

-He becomes the only person to win both Wrestler and MVP in the same year.
-He tagged with Bobby Eaton as "Midnight Gold" and placed in RRO Top 10.
-He was voted "Valentine King" in 1983 in Salem, IL
-For the last two years, he has won every award that he has been nominated for.

## RRO TOP 10 OF THE YEAR 2010

**TAG TEAMS**
10: "Too Cruel" [Brian Christopher/Wolfe D]
9: "CCR" [Demon X/Wild Bill]
8: Dell Tucker/Rockin Randy
7: "East Coast Bad Boys" [Spyro/C-Money]
6: "SNS" [Syn/Stunner]
5: "Midnight Gold" [Bobby Eaton/Greg Anthony]
4: "LSD" [Idol Bane/Cody Only/Deadly Dale]
3: "Premiere Brutality" [Kid Nikels/Eric Wayne]
2: "Picture Perfect" [Jon Michael/Christian Jacobs]

# 1: "Asylum" [Psycho/Pappy]

SINGLES

10: Matt Riviera
9: Gary Valiant
8: Pokerface
7: Christian Jacobs
6: Jon Michael
5: Stan Lee
4: Derrick King
3: Alan Steele
2: Austin Lane

# 1: Greg Anthony

## AUTOGRAPH PAGE

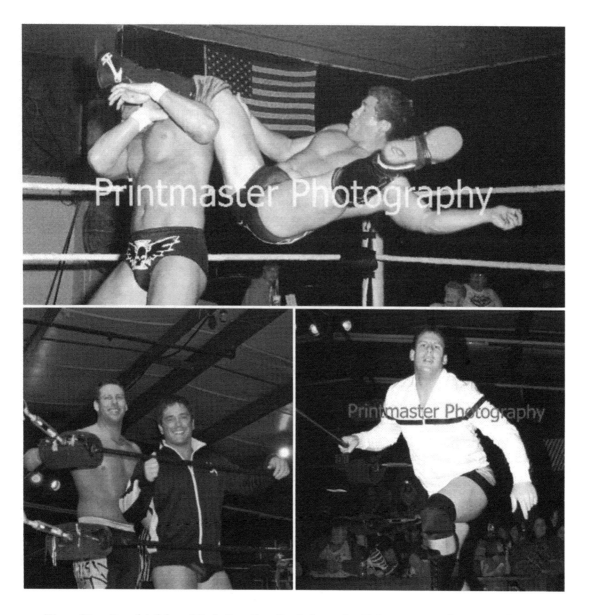

**Top: Stan Lee kicking Christian Jacobs [photo by Printmaster photography Rick Nelson]**

**Botton: Chris O'Neal/Stan Lee and Chris O'Neal [photo by Printmaster photography Rick Nelson]**

## AUTOGRAPH PAGE

Top row from left: Austin Lane, Brian Thompson and Matt Riviera

Bottom from left: Garry White, Ron Horn celebrating four years of RRO and Frankie Tucker

# RRO MEMPHIS WRESTLING

# HALL OF FAME

# CLASS OF 2010

## By Brian Thompson

The 2010 Class of the RRO Memphis Hall of Fame

By Brian Thompson

No wrestling historian could ever doubt the impact that the Memphis Wrestling territory has had on the world of professional wrestling throughout the years. And the 2010 class of the RasslinRiotOnline Memphis Hall of Fame features a variety of superstars who would leave their mark in various ways on the "sport of kings" at local, regional, national and even global levels.

Each year a combination of those involved in the wrestling business and wrestling experts, who are all most importantly wrestling fans at heart, come together to decide the inductees into the RRO Memphis Hall of Fame.

All participants inducted into the Hall are basically retired from a full-time schedule, although they may be active on a part-time basis. Members of the Hall must also be at least 35-years-old with 10 or more years of "Major League" wrestling experience or it has been at least 15 years since his or her debut as a full-time performer. The Hall will include singles wrestlers, tag teams, announcers, bookers, promoters and managers.

This year's Hall of Fame section of the RRO Yearbook will include a biography of each inductee that includes comments from Mike Lano, a wrestling writer, photographer and radio host since 1966; wrestling enthusiast Steve Crawford, and wrestling personality Oscar Barlow.

With the formalities out of the way, let's take a look at the 2010 class of the RRO Memphis Hall of Fame.

CLASS OF 2010

| | |
|---|---|
| The Nightmares – Danny Davis & Ken Wayne | Downtown Bruno |
| Buddy Wayne | Dave Brown |
| Robert Fuller | The Moondogs with Richard Lee |
| "Macho Man" Randy Savage | "Mouth of the South" Jimmy Hart |

**THE NIGHTMARES**

**(DANNY DAVIS & KEN WAYNE)**

**Photo by Mike Lano wrealano@aol.com**

If "The Nightmares" had listened to any critic that says "size matters," then the world of professional wrestling would have missed out on a unique combination that was ahead of its time.

While others, such as Ted Allen, have been labeled with the "Nightmare" name, most experts consider the true "Nightmares" to be Ken Wayne, a second generation wrestler, and Danny Davis, who achieved some of his initial success as a manager. When Wayne and Davis, who first competed together under masks before losing the hoods for painted "stars" on their faces, began teaming it was like they had always teamed together.

"The tag team combination, two smaller workers that performed like a well oiled machine, were ahead of their time," said Steve Crawford, a wrestling enthusiast. "What they lacked in size, they made up for in quickness, skill and timing. They performed perfectly as a unit, setting the stage for the success of future tag teams that emphasized speed and teamwork, such as the Rock N' Roll Express and the Fantastics."

Throughout their career, they earned championship gold earning stints as the Southern Tag Team Champions with a 1984 defeat of Ricky Morton & Robert Gibson as well as numerous Southern Tag Team titles and Continental Tag Team crowns.

"In addition to working in Memphis, they were often headliners in the Continental area and they taught Jimmy Cornette the tricks of managing an effective team when they worked as the Galaxians," said Crawford.

Brian Thompson, local wrestling personality and journalist, noted that the team had the ability to give fans a more entertaining match, even at times when they were asked to put over another duo.

"One of my favorite Ken Wayne stories is the one he tells of a match he and Danny had with the Bobby Eaton and Stan Lane version of the Midnight Express," said Thompson. "It was a television taping for WTBS and most fans expected a straight squash. A combination of Eaton and Lane's realization that you are only as good as the opposition that you beat plus the 'Nightmares' abilities provided that crowd with a memorable match and Wayne noted that crowd gave he and Danny applause on the way back to the lockerroom following the bout."

While they left a legacy of quality in-ring work with everyone they ever competed against or with, the "Nightmares" final legacy may be in the athletes that they create for the future.

"Both continue their wrestling legacy by having two of the most well-respected training programs in the business," said Crawford.

Wayne runs the "Nightmare Ken Wayne School of Professional Wrestling" located in West Memphis, AR. As part of the school, trainees have a chance to appear on "New Experience Wrestling," a televised wrestling promotion that also operates out of the school and has television clearance in Mississippi. For more information on the school, visit www.nightmarekenwayne.com or call (901) 831-4198.

As his in-ring career winded down, Davis began Ohio Valley Wrestling and a training school that have produced some of wrestling's business superstars in the last two decades. For many years, OVW was a World Wrestling Federation, now known as World Wrestling Entertainment, developmental territory. Through its contractual agreement, OVW provided its services to help create the stars of tomorrow for the WWE. Trainers were hired by WWE and OVW had multiple television clearances in the Lousiville, KY area. After the WWE pulled its contract with OVW, Davis survived some tough years to recently begin a working agreement with Ring of Honor (ROH), bringing that organization's style of wrestling to the city while also continuing to develop stars for the future.

**Phil Hickerson and Downtown Burno**

DOWNTOWN BRUNO

As far as Downtown Bruno being in the 2010 Class of the RRO Memphis Hall of Fame, let's just say that "Mama Says it Beez That Way Sometimes."

"Downtown Bruno Lauer is going to be one of our top Cauliflower Alley Club honorees next year in Las Vegas (www.caulifloweralleyclub.org) along with top people he knows well in Mick Foley and Jim Ross, to name a few," said Mike Lano, wrestling writer, photographer and radio host around the globe since 1966. "While most would be familiar with his WWF exploits, his true workload was working for genius Jerry Jarrett of course. Whether cutting hilarious promos, managing, or even getting involved in a variety of creative ways, Bruno never disappointed."

After getting his initial start in Mississippi and then in the northeastern part of the country, Bruno made his way to the Memphis territory and became the top manager for the Jerry Jarrett/Jerry Lawler owned promotion. He led his heel charges in an effort to bring down Lawler from the throne of "King" in Memphis. Bruno was also highly successful for the Fullers in Continental Wrestling even winning the organization's United States Junior Heavyweight Title.

Bruno's career break came in 1991 when he was hired by the World Wrestling Federation and renamed "Harvey Wippleman." As the next in a long line of devious managers, Bruno led such stars as Big Bully Busick, Sid Vicious, Kamala, Well Dunn and Bertha Faye, among others. The Walls, MS, resident reached the pinnacle in April 1992 when he managed Vicious against Hulk Hogan in one of two main events as part of WrestleMania VIII at the Hoosier Dome in Indianapolis. One year later, while not in the main event of the show, he was the manager of Giant Gonzales in a match against future legend The Undertaker. It was Undertaker's second win in his now infamous undefeated streak at wrestling's biggest event of the year.

At SummerSlam 1995, Bruno led Bertha Faye to the WWF World Women's Championship with a victory over Alundra "Madusa" Blayze. During the same year, Bruno battled legendary WWF ring announcer Howard "The Fink" Finkel in a tuxedo match. It would not be Bruno's last "wrestling" appearance for the company, as four years later he defeated The Kat to win the WWF World Women's Title.

"While Bobby Heenan was more infamously known as the 'Weasel,' it is truly the perfect moniker for Fort Duquesne Boulevard's sneaky, underhanded Downtown Bruno," said Steve Crawford. "Bruno was insufferably obnoxious with zero redeeming qualities in his managerial role. He was great on the mic and was one of the last Memphis managers to generate real heat with the fans. Bruno got his start working small independent shows in Pennsylvania and made it all the way to managing Sid Vicious as the headliner at WrestleMania VIII against Hulk Hogan!"

"I have known him for 20 years," said Oscar Barlow, local wrestling personality. "USWA was having a show in my hometown in May 1996. I was mayor of Crenshaw, MS. I was going to wrestle Scott Bowden, but he had left the area. So my first and last match was with Bruno. Since then we have remained friends. I still do announcing for shows and we keep in touch. I just appointed him a special police officer for Crenshaw, MS. He is a class act."

Bruno continues to work for WWE in a backstage capacity and recently completed his autobiography entitled "Wrestling with the Truth," which received universal acclaim from those within the business and fans alike.

In addition, Bruno has always found ways to "give back" to the business through his participation with local organizations. He has helped mold and shaped stars in the USWA, Power Pro Wrestling, Arkansas All-Star Wrestling and, most recently, New Experience Wrestling where he can be seen as a referee on most Friday nights in West Memphis, AR, at the "Nightmare Ken Wayne School of Professional Wrestling."

**BUDDY WAYNE**

Saying "he's done it all in the world of wrestling" is something that gets tossed around far too often. But that 9-word phrase pretty much sums up the career of the legendary Buddy Wayne, whose legacy lives on through his son and grandson.

Buddy spent many years mastering his craft through travels around the world in the "territory days" of professional wrestling.

"Buddy Wayne was a student of the game, who thoroughly understood the business and ring psychology," said Steve Crawford. "A solid hand in the ring, Buddy also made a significant impact as a promoter and a trainer."

One of the most exciting times in his career came when Buddy had the opportunity to team with his son Ken. The Wayne duo had a fun run feuding with a fellow father-son combination of Tommy and Eddie Gilbert. This early feud set both Ken and Eddie on their ways in what would become successful careers of their own. Having fathers in the sport certainly helped their cause as the fathers understood the need to make their sons "pay proper dues" before stepping into the ring.

After his in-ring career came to a conclusion, Buddy continued to be a valuable asset to the sport as a promoter. He promoted numerous towns for the Memphis Wrestling territory. His legacy lives on through his son Ken and now his grandson – "3G" Eric Wayne.

Friendly 5: Lance and Dave were a Saturday morning institution on Channel 5.

## DAVE BROWN photo by Jason Plank

In the comic books and movies Batman had Robin and the legendary announcer Lance Russell had Dave Brown, the next inductee into the RRO Memphis Hall of Fame, for Saturday morning wrestling telecasts.

Brown has been a fixture in the Memphis area as a weatherman for WMC TV-5 in the city, a position he still prominently holds. But for wrestling fans in the region, on Saturday morning he was Russell's sidekick for the "calls of the action" in the WMC TV-5 studio.

"Dave Brown was the perfect color man compliment to the state-of-the-art Lance Russell and later on his own with Corey Maclin," said Mike Lano. "A guy with legit broadcasting credentials who enjoyed his time in wrestling behind the mic, never giving off a (Tony) Schiavone-type condescending attitude and making the product believable and compelling."

"While Lance Russell served as the master of ceremonies for what was often a three ring circus in Memphis Wrestling, Dave Brown provided a calm logical voice," said Steve Crawford. "As the weatherman on WMC TV, the same station that aired the wrestling program, Dave had instant credibility with the Memphis television audience. His understated delivery worked perfectly with Lance's well honed incredulous disbelief ('for crying out loud!'). Memphis never had a better tag team than Lance and Dave."

Brown became almost one of the "faces of Memphis Wrestling" along with Jerry "The King" Lawler, Russell and "Superstar" Bill Dundee. He was with the USWA until its final year and then returned to the scene when Randy Hales created "Power Pro Wrestling." A recognizable face and personality in the city of Memphis, Brown has shown that he has a caring spirit with his involvement in important causes.

"I was first introduced to Dave by Lance Russell," said Oscar Barlow. "Lance and I had been friends for awhile. Lance had a radio show on 95.3 working for Eddie Bond. Lance had invited me to WMC-TV for the Saturday morning show. Since then, Dave and I have been in touch. We all prayed for Dave and his family during the death of his daughter and grandchildren. Dave does great work with MADD (Mothers Against Drunk Driving). He is still the No. 1 weatherman in the area and is also a class act."

Brian Thompson said that he always appreciated Dave's ability to take wrestling seriously, unlike others who come from other forms of broadcasting.

"A lot of times you get a radio DJ or someone who thinks they can announce wrestling because they do similar work in some other form of entertainment," said Thompson. "It is not that easy. Dave never came across as a weatherman calling wrestling. You could easily convince someone that he was a full-time wrestling commentator and that was all he did, he was that good at it. I'll never forget one instance of his attention to detail. It was on a Saturday morning show a couple of years ago when it was a taped show with Dave, Lawler and Corey Maclin introducing clips. Well, there was a storm that morning and Dave had to cut in live from the studios. To make the wrestling show seem 'live,' he said that he was able to change clothes and get to the studio to do the weather. Now THAT is attention to detail."

**ROBERT FULLER**

**Photo by Mike Lano wrealano@aol.com**

When it comes to Tennessee wrestling there is only one stud – "The Tennessee Stud" Robert Fuller, who wrestled all over the world on many stages during his illustrious career as a wrestler, manager and promoter.

"Robert Fuller wrestled virtually everywhere," said Mike Lano. "Obviously (he wrestled) in the Southeast with great efforts also in Florida and Georgia and even at the Kiel (St. Louis, MO). Some of the memorable Atlanta City Auditorium cards I shot in '73 and '74 there always involved his ultimate babyface team with Bob Armstrong. What a legend and from a total legendary family that resembles the Anoia/Samoans in terms of reach."

"His grandfather Roy Welch partnered with Nick Gulas as a wrestling promoter in Tennessee," said Steve Crawford. "His father Buddy Fuller was a professional wrestler throughout the 1960s and early 1970s. Robert is also the brother of wrestler/promoter Ron Fuller and the cousin of Jimmy Golden. Robert worked for years in the Georgia, Alabama and Tennessee territories and was a top regional star. He had the size to look credible against anyone in the ring and he was an outstanding interview in his smart aleck, heel persona. After two decades in the ring, he had a successful run in World Championship Wrestling (WCW) in his managerial role as Col. Robert Parker."

**THE MOONDOGS WITH RICHARD LEE   Photo by Mike Lano wrealano@aol.com**

If the Moondogs were still alive to receive a physical plaque for their induction into the RRO Memphis Hall of Fame, all other attendees would be encouraged to run because the plaque and anything else not tied down was fair game for use as a weapon! The Moondogs, along with their early 1990s manager Richard Lee, were "hardcore" before that was even a term in the world of professional wrestling and their style of brawling against fan favorites such as Jerry Lawler and Jeff Jarrett revitalized the Memphis territory in the early part of the 1990s.

"Don Laible and I actually shot (photos of) Richard Lee managing the Moondogs in several '92 Tennessee great cards and whether heel or face, the crowd ate them up too," said Mike Lano.

"The Moondogs were part of some of the wildest brawls in the history of Memphis Wrestling, which is no small accomplishment," said Steve Crawford. "The first set of Moondogs to invade the territory were Moondogs Spot (Larry Latham) and Rex (Randy Colley), who had some legendary matches with the Fabulous Ones. In the early 1990s, with the Memphis territory doing slow business, Moondogs Spot, Cujo,/Splat (Cousin Junior) and Spike (Bill Smithson) were brought into the promotion to gnaw on some bones. The Moondogs had wild melees with Jerry Lawler and Jeff Jarrett, which not only brought back the fans, but won the 'Feud of the Year' in the 'Wrestling Observer Newsletter.' Whenever manager Richard Lee started blowing his whistle, the fans knew some devastating action was about to occur."

**"MACHO MAN" RANDY SAVAGE**

**Photo by Mike Lano wrealano@aol.com**

As far as the RRO Memphis Hall of the Fame is concerned, the debate is over! "The Macho Man" is in the Hall of Fame!

"Randy Savage – 'nuff said," said Mike Lano. "It would be trivial to say he's done it all, but he has. His best athletic work was of course for (Jerry) Jarrett and the loved guilty pleasure of the Poffo's Kentucky ICW promotion which was ahead of its time and a bit of a predecessor to ECW's thumbing it's nose at everyone else a decade and a half later. His work in mains ala against Lawler, Dundee, Dutch Mantell was awesome as was his equally great tag work with his brother against the Rock and Rolls, etc. I'm surprised he wasn't in here already."

"The Macho Man was one of the most colorful characters in professional wrestling," said Steve Crawford. "Randy and the Poffo family became known to Memphis Wrestling fans through their outlaw ICW promotion, which aired on Memphis television. The promotion survived on a shoestring budget for years, featuring performers who would later become major stars in WCW and WWF, such as the One Man Gang (Crusher Broomfield) and Ronnie Garvin. When ICW closed shop, the Poffo family came into the Memphis promotion. Savage had been challenging Memphis wrestlers on the air for years while working for ICW, so he was immediately booked into a successful program with Jerry Lawler. Incredibly intense, both in interviews and in the ring, Savage exuded tremendous charisma and confidence. He would later go on to have an incredibly successful and long run in the World Wrestling Federation, holding the WWF Championship twice."

**"MOUTH OF THE SOUTH" JIMMY HART**

**Photo by Mike Lano wrealano@aol.com**

We certainly saved one of the best for lasts in professional wrestling's true "ambassador" Jimmy Hart, who for years drew the ire of wrestling fans worldwide after making his big mark in Memphis.

"Jimmy Hart is the ultimate guy who can walk into any locker room and add something," said Mike Lano. "And not get kicked out! Who else in a span of a week can waltz right into a WWE, TNA, ROH and indy locker room without a peep from anyone and instead be welcomed with open arms? From his Gentries musical career we're all aware of, to all the stuff he did in Memphis, to being one of the highlights of Ole bringing back Georgia Championship Wrestling in the early Saturday morning hours after WWF's Black Friday managing the Dirty White Boys on an international stage for the first time which caught the eye of Pat and others in WWF, leading to big time stuff in Connecticut and later WCW, his own promotion with Hogan in Florida, back to WWE's locker room and TNA! Jimmy Hart, like Jim Cornette, loves the biz relentlessly and it shows. A true historian, super guy in private and still a proud "mark for the business." Jimmy Hart is the best for those of us proud to call him a friend and it's a pleasure to see him inducted into this Hall of Fame."

After his musical success, Hart befriended Jerry Lawler leading to his run as "The King's" manager. That relationship went sour when Hart turned on Lawler after Lawler suffered an injury. The two did serious box office business with Lawler facing multiple charges led by Hart, including Andy Kaufman in the legendary 1982 fued.

RasslinRiotOnline.com endorses two professional wrestling schools based in the Mid South.

## The "Nightmare" Ken Wayne School of Professional Wrestling

Based in West Memphis, AR, the "Nightmare" Ken Wayne School of Professional Wrestling provides a thorough education for those who want to become involved in wrestling. Various levels of instruction are offered for wrestlers, managers, and referees, and for those who may already be involved in the business.

The school began in 2006, less than one year after Ken Wayne retired as an active performer to totally pursue the new operation.

Two athletes – Ken's son Eric Wayne and Kevin "Kid" Nikels – have completed the school, following a 1-hour graduation match in February 2008. That match won RRO Arena Match of the Year 2008. Greg King, Jr competed this year in his graduation match.

As an additional form of education for his students, Ken started New Experience Wrestling in October 2008. The promotion allows his trainees to learn the in's and out's of how to perform on a live to tape television show, and they also discover how the show is produced from a technological standpoint.

For more information on the school, visit www.nightmarekenwayne.com or call (901) 831-4198.

## Kevin White's Wrestling School

Kevin White's Wrestling School is located in Jackson, TN, and provides its students with outstanding opportunities through the knowledge provided by head trainer Kevin White.

In recent years, Kevin has become a breakout star in the Mid South. He has been a fixture on Memphis Wrestling's weekly TV show, seen by thousands of fans in the region over the years. Trained by "Superstar" Bill Dundee, Kevin is now providing many of the crucial skills he learned to the future of wrestling in the Mid South.

Su Yung, The Gladiator; Maxx Corbin, Albino Rhino; and Cody Melton are three of the most notable performers to come from the school. Sue was a featured performer during the final few months of Memphis Wrestling's run of original programming on CW-30 in late 2007. She was named the area's top female performer by peers, experts, and fans of RasslinRiotOnline in 2010.

Their success is a testament to the kind of skills that Kevin White teaches at his school.

For more information on the school, visit www.MySpace.com/kevinwhite76.

Photo credits

----I usually credit every single photo in the book with each page number.  AND, I screw up majorly, because the Yearbook is done in three or four stages.  So...this year...I am just listing the people who provided pics [unless otherwise noted].  Thanks to all and I appreciate it!!

**Donna Pardee**

**Tia Blaylock**

**Brian Tramel**

**Kayte Tramel**

**Karly Tramel**

**Rick Nelson**

**Christy Shaw**

**Myspace/Facebook profiles**

**John Coffin**

**Mike Lano**

**TGB Cover and various TGB shots: Joshua Mashon**

7229472R0

Made in the USA
Charleston, SC
06 February 2011